A JOURNEY OF POSSIBILITIES

Are those possibilities restricted by the systems design and programs? Who controls the game?

"For the human body to live 250,000 years is not a miracle, neither is it an impossible dream, neither is it a ridiculous idea. Your memory of a life not bound by time was altered and such limiting perceptions took the forefront, streaming such limiting codes from our DNA. Despite this illusion of limitation our DNA remains unlimited in its access beyond time and space; an endless stream of codes and data. We have been bamboozled into believing that a long life will be pointless as we no longer remember that such timeless bodies were occupied by minds capable of building new concepts and new models of this virtual playground."

Sonia Barrett

TIMELINE PUBLISHING INC.,
North Hollywood, CA

Contents

INTRODUCTION

A Journey of Possibilities is a collection of a select few of the most stimulating articles that I have written over the course of a few years. Each one is like its own unique book covering a diverse range of information in each. Perhaps you may have already read some of these articles. However having them compiled in this format will allow the reader to conveniently reference each one again and again.

Each article is so rich with stimulating ideas and concepts that reading them more than once will reveal layers of coded information. So it is will most all reading material. We see and read just a small fraction of what is actually there. Because of this what we find is that we may reread a book or other reading material only to discover information that we have no recollection of having read previously. It is amazing how much is missed. It is for this reason that it is suggested that you read and come back to the same material perhaps in a day or even a week or longer and you will discover information that you had not read before. Or perhaps you may have an evolution in your interpretation of the material in your second reading.

It is necessary that we push the envelope in our thinking. Operating in the safety of our beliefs can greatly retard or limit the kind of evolution that we might be seeking. This collection of insights examines possibilities, our way of thinking and our beliefs and the system of reality around us. You are encouraged to come out of hiding in terms of who you truly are. The virtual and programmed nature of reality becomes clear in many of these writings and that alone is encouragement in realizing that there is no need to live up to the expectations of others. These are all programmed beliefs. Fear of ridicule or of standing alone in one's truth or in one's curiosity is an illusion. You lose nothing by being who you truly are. In the end people don't really care what you do or what you believe at least not as much as you are lead to believe that they do. Everyone one is busy complying and blending in perhaps as much as you are.

Standing in our truth doesn't mean that we must impose those truths on others. When we are truly confident in who were are there is no need or desire to battle with others about their truths.

It is my hope that perhaps daily you may connect with information in these pages that will lead you to yet a deeper level of you. Spiritual expansion is about deeper thought and deeper thought creates a sense of freedom. Perhaps with that sense of freedom one will begin to see that there really are no gates only the programs and beliefs by which our lives have been shaped. Enjoy the adventure!

Sonia Barrett

1

Collective Conditioning and the Mechanics of Reality

Coming up for air from the challenges of our life's stories is a pursued reward. This seemingly simple desire can actually be a challenging accomplishment for many. The truth is that our life is built on our story, whatever that may be, regardless of the conditions that led to that story. We are generally submerged in this experience on a daily basis. We are addicts to our lives, although we yearn to be relieved of these experiences. In our heads we chant our likes and dislikes in a very unconscious ritual. We run pictures and images through our minds as a confirmation and validation of these selected stores.

There seems to be no end to this torment. Time is then assigned as the scale of "value", for if we are to live these stories in our heads, we must become fully immersed in the "time" construct. Our ability to modify the dimension of time is part of the misunderstood magic, for what we are able to do in our minds we can also do in the outward version of reality. In our minds, we are able to live two weeks or ten years in but just a moment. However, we are faced with collective conditioning and our addiction to such beliefs about the mechanics of reality. We ultimately exist in the realm of imagination...who or what is imagining us? Are we the ultimate imaginer? Why are we so afraid to own that position? Perhaps it is because, for so long, we have been convinced that someone else is at the wheel. This has allowed us the luxury of blaming something outside of our self. What's outside...we are both outside and inside. If that is the case, then where can blame ultimately be placed?

There is no doubt that within the intricate layers of reality, are worlds and realms of opposing and allied forces, where we are both stalked and assisted. Those ascended and descended, planetary life and alien life, dimensions and planets light years away; all exists under the umbrella of time, for it requires the condensing or expanding of time in order to travel within these spaces. Is time than simply an imagined concept or a stage to play out our stories? Many speak of shifts, but a shift into what exactly? Is it more of the familiar collective dream neatly wrapped in a more expansive version of our limitations and protocols? This may seem like a contradiction, but it is very possible to add scope to one's limitations. Noticing these ongoing limitations can be challenging, especially when one's environment continues to reaffirm this position.

We should keep in mind that reality and science are only as final as our perception dictates. So in order to come up for air, and to deeply breathe in freedom, we must be reminded of our stories and of the magic of our imagination; image-in-action or magic in action. Snap out of the dream (at least for a moment). Time is a marketed concept and the manner in which you choose to interact with it is up to each of us. Oneness is also about uniqueness and our ability as individuals to stretch the envelope. Without minds willing to move forward in this manner, one may continue to feel imprisoned in this reality mind trap. The key is to question your life and your stories. You represent the whole, and your obligation is to be unlimited in your imagination...your own unique imagination. Oneness and separateness are a paradox, so we must live both by being all that we deem possible without the restrictions of conclusive analysis about the nature of reality. Just live!

2

Time table" of the Robot/Character: The Calendar 12/12/12 OR 12/21/12

This 3rd dimensional experience is of a virtual nature exemplifying the life of the character. We have wholly defined and identified ourselves as the character. It is the character's existence that is measurable and finite. The "character" is a mere avatar in this virtual playground.

Definition of Avatar (Webster Dictionary):

1. *A variant phase or version of a continuing basic entity*

2. *An electronic image that represents and is manipulated by a computer user (as in a computer game)*

To simply assess that we are spiritual beings, having a human experience does not adequately summarize what is taking place, yet paradoxically it does. The challenge with this concept is that it is trivialized, or minimally decoded, in our thinking and so we continue to see ourselves as the character. The character is, however, clever in disguising itself as a spiritual being having a human experience. Confused? In life there is a role that is being played no differently than the role played in a play or film. That role is defined by the character and is the character. It is the character that is afraid of his/her demise. The thought of not existing, or of being able to play on the stage of life, is the character's greatest fear. The actor; the character; lives in an awareness of its dispensable fate. However, we are fooled into believing that the character's fear expresses the totality of what we are, because in our 3rd dimensional thinking we are vulnerable to annihilation at any moment. The character's power is, however, limited to the dual nature of the mind. The character splits off into two minds; one focuses on keeping the game of limitation going and the other realizes that, ultimately, power must be relinquished to the grander essence, its co-partner throughout the journey.

The character will hold out and keep the game going until it is forced to accept new directions. It's a rather schizophrenic process occurring; a multiple personality dis-order, one that serves the purpose of the journey. From the complex space of the character, everything about the character's world is run by programs, a vast storage of data used as reference points for decision making. Choice points of a repetitious nature streaming from the collective history of human programs. This history is the collective human character's experiences ranging from war to peace. Planetary annihilation has occurred in numerous versions of earth, all recorded in the memory bank of humans and embedded in the human program. This confusion about the ending of the world, based on dates and times, relates to the reality of the character. Our attachment to the measurability of the span of life is related to the vulnerability of the character. The character's existence is given value and measured through the survival and animation of the human body. The calendar and all such time defining components are in place to map and to navigate the life of the character. That which we are beyond the body and the character exceeds the measurability of time and space. Therefore, decisions regarding the longevity of the character are decided by its copartner, producer and director of the character's script. On its own, the character can only operate from memory and programmed content. The lifespan of the character is measured by the evolution of the character's role. (When the character/robot self has exceeded its programmed and ritualistic responses evolution has begun requiring new concepts and ideas not limited to a conditioned set of beliefs and programs.)

The barometer of time is then an essential element in establishing a platform up on which the temporal nature the character will play. Through the character, or robot self, the human game can be experienced. For some, the world will end on 12/12/12 or 12/21/12, as people seem to die perhaps more excessively of unexpected or unexplainable circumstances. Each human carries a code that plugs into certain time cycles. Some are coded to be here and cross the threshold into 2013 the same as all other times. What we are dealing with are program streams related to the cycles of planet earth, and what each specific version of earth is wired for. Although it's a comforting belief that we are operating in a consistent or static reality, it's necessary to entertain the thought that from moment-to-moment reality changes despite its apparent visual familiarity. The version of earth we each experience is not necessarily the only expression of earth. Who's to say whether you have been planted on the same reality of earth since embodying this human experience? Life is a great paradox; nothing is real, yet everything is. This understanding makes everything possible. The reality we encounter is contingent on the latitude given. For as we operate from a place of greater latitude, our individual conscious, beliefs, and possibilities are stretched and the longevity of one's character, or avatar, is no longer vulnerable to the whims of the game, but can play indefinitely while merging into more evolved modules of the cosmic game. Eventually the character disappears into the expanded self.

The Mayan calendar is a simplified system of the astrological navigation system or map, which supports the journey of the character/robot self through the programs. Consciousness, as it relates to the character/automated/robotic self, is steered through its evolution via the cyclic systems. The year 2012 is said to be the end of the world and it is from one perspective. There is an ending to particular components in the operating system as it relates to the needs of humanity for the next level of evolution in this virtual game system; the system we appear to share collectively. This can be considered and upgraded to the system. The impact of the upgrade is contingent on the reality journal of each being.

How we direct our characters through the experience will depend on making a conscious distinction between the writer, producer, director, and the character; then time cycles will no longer be the illusionary decider of our fate. When such a realization is born or truly awakened in us and we own it, time, calendars and cycles will no longer be the feared assailant chasing us. You are time chasing yourself in the programmed matrix of the universe, aging and dying according to the rules of the game that we have chosen to play. It's challenging at times to conceive that one would create such a game. Once the true memory of this illusory process comes alive in us, we will no longer despise the game. Neither will we ask why we would have stepped into these virtual gears. To become free of these limitations is to learn the art of reading life for every moment presents clues and codes to the programs and agreements to which we continue to hold allegiance.

It is the character that ages and dies. It is the character, the robot-self whose life hinges on the cyclically run calendar. Simulation after simulation; Will the world end, or will it continue? Which simulation of earth are you coded for? What are your belief systems? How much of your focus is invested in fear of planetary annihilation? Go on and plan for tomorrow, for life is but a dream. We experience life through a series of smoke and mirrors throughout the course of the game, and as we stop to engage, they become part of our reality. Examine your hang-ups and your spiritual beliefs, and if your conclusion is fear, and possible annihilation, then ask yourself by whose rules are you playing the game of life. Examine the programs of your character, your avatar; perhaps it's time to reprogram. Remember that you are both the player and the game itself, so no matter what happens, you will always exist. You are the fabric upon which you create and play!

3

The Infiltration of Tragedy on the Collective
The season, the media, and your emotional response

There is an infiltration to the minds and to the emotions of collective consciousness. Globally, this time of year is celebrated in various ways, in many cultures. The fact is that there is a frequency of joy or happiness during this season. This is the expected frequency of the season. Despite personal feelings and emotional challenges…the season represents a joyous/happy frequency or vibration. When opposing frequencies, which are exact opposite of joy and happiness, are savagely injected into our reality; during these times, it scrambles the human mind. There is emotional confusion to the psyche. We are collectively scrambled. There is fear, sadness with shades of happiness as deep down we are naturally wired to engage in the joy of the season.

When children are harmed, it impacts the emotional field more strongly, especially when there are severe degrees of brutality. We are traumatized in a way that we are unable to process. People are left trying to figure out where to place their emotions. There is guilt for being happy while others mourn.

Reality does not operate on coincidences but rather a series of event resulting in each new outcome. Because life is a grand game we must remember that life is viewed and played through the eyes of the character. Characters have damaged or virus ridden programs. Humans are capable of immeasurable levels of wickedness and goodness. Because of this, when we are chemically scrambled by certain substances, such as pharmaceuticals, or when we are emotionally shattered, or perhaps when the brain has connecting issues then any assortment of emotional responses and actions become possible. Human emotions are very fragile as we are dependent on electrochemical impulses to process and to experience the sensations of reality. In the game of our world, minds are experimented on, yielding the most significant results from the extremely fragile and vulnerable minds. The mind of the weak is a susceptive environment for establishing defragmenting programs.

In light of the resent tragedies, the media will continue to repeatedly show pictures as tragic events are turned into a movie on a moment-to-moment basis. We watch it over and over while our minds and emotions are taken over. Collectively, we are integrated into the tragic experience. Repeatedly inundating our minds with replays of any tragedy is the fastest, and perhaps the simplest, way to navigate the collective into a common bandwidth, and from their collective inserts and programming can more efficiently be administered. We won't be the wiser as we are automatically and emotionally online (reality matrix feed) at the same time. It is the energy of the collective that is used to power reality in whatever shape it takes. So ideally, in order to direct that power source to support the desired form or function of reality, it is necessary that there is a convergence of the collective in an appropriate level of resonance or output.

While the mentally ill may walk the streets of all cities, it is not them that seem to reign down tragedy. These mass killings are generally carried out by the educated, and according to the media, brilliant minds; honor roll and exceptional students, but generally troubled minds. These are never the mentally ill living on the street.
The new year/cycle is coming and, as always, minds are prepped with tragedy as we are reminded in the media that the "nation mourns". Most often, this kind of collective jarring occurs right after the first of the year with tragic occurrences that rocks the world. Many were already making their way into 2013, shaken by personal tragedies and now the collective has also been imprinted. When trauma is trapped in the body and the mind, this gives rise to a great many illness that may plague or ravage the body. How many people will be cancer ridden in the coming year? How many will develop

heart problems because their hearts are broken? How many will become crippled by fear as we look to our leaders to protect us? How much more of our personal freedom will we surrender in light of these events? Although there is pain, we must find a way to process this, if not, we will become consumed by it. And should our bodies succumb to these imbalances, we will not be the wiser about when it all started.

Remember that children are also beings who have come here with their own unique map and agreements etc., we must not lose sight of this as we shift into a space of compassion...not to be confused with pity. These are tough moments, but we must become aware of the journey we take, being aware of how 2013 is being shaped into our personal reality. This is the dance of the character. How we store these tragedies will shape and imprint us as individuals and as a collective. Change the shape of your current paradigm by changing your perception of the external playground. Have compassion, but make your gift to the external world a shift in perception. Release the guilt and override opposing energies by authentically experiencing joy this season with family and friends, as many will be unable to do so.

4

Removing the Shackles of the Game
"Do not go gently into that good night without a fight"

The game of living consists of an assortment of expressions; we exemplify life by expressing and experimenting ideas through play. We dance upon the stage of life with our scripts and characters. We breathe life into these ideas and soon the creator becomes the created. The character comes to life and takes over. We become prisoners of these characters and soon our game becomes a warzone. Life is then defined by the interaction between characters. We watch and observe from behind our eyes as characters battle for survival. The game seems to grow with increasing conflicts. Conflict does not necessarily entail an obvious struggle, but can encompass much subtlety as we succumb to the role of the character. It's all so believable.

Who or what is the character? Like everything else, it is an idea being acted upon; it is an idea being played out. We have defined ourselves by these ideas from which we construct storylines. This all becomes the face of reality for each of us. These bodies are idea streamers. Through them, we are able to experience particular concepts of possibilities, one of which we refer to as the 3rd dimension. There is no permanency to these idea streams as they are convertible and interchangeable for new idea streams and possibilities. We are, however, challenged by yet another idea or belief of fixed or irreversible idea patterns. The game is made up of a series of idea patterns also known as frequency patterns; nothing fixed or permanent. It's a synthesizing experience.

"The world of matter is a relative world, and an illusory one, illusory not in the sense that it does not exist, but illusory in the sense that we do not see it as it really is. The way it really is cannot be communicated verbally, but in the attempt to talk around it, eastern literature speaks repeatedly of dancing energy and transient impermanent forms. This is strikingly similar to the picture of physical reality emerging from high-energy particle physics. Buddhist literature does not speak of learning new things about reality, but about removing veils of ignorance that stand between us and what we already are." - Gary Zukav, Dancing Wu Li Masters

Although we may strongly desire to understand more about this life, as experienced in these bodies and even beyond the body; we are continuously being rerouted and redirected into deeper pockets of the game. The depths of distractions through which we are routed create extensive distance between the limited and the unlimited. Much of these limitations are delivered to us via the spiritual journey. To become lost in the idea of spirituality as a mystical experience, attainable only by the select, is yet another mind trap. Spirituality is about an endless remembering and of a reintegration of these memories as they unfold. We are all spiritual beings living life through these characters we have created. Despite being lost in these characters, we must realize that the stories through which these characters operate are fully encoded with clues and codes, guiding us to our own extraction or emergence from the game. We are generally immersed in the featured story in our life at this very moment, and once we are immersed, we become the story which seems to grow tentacles, pulling us in even deeper.

Spirituality is not just about becoming a socially or spiritually defined "good person". It is about *being* what you need to be as you explore your way to authenticity. Since the clues to unlocking yourself lies in your own stories it is then necessary to follow your own trail. This is not to say that we can't be assisted and guided by others. It is about feeling what feels right for you in that moment. It is about feeling what resonates. What are your fears? Some cling to spiritual ideas coddling feel-good tales of saviors and of an escape to other realms supporting peace. We are driven to be on the run. This isn't about running, but rather about discovering that there is nothing to run from. We are being chased by experiences built into our version of reality. How we view those experiences greatly determine how or if we shift beyond them.

"In much of these spiritual movements, there are limitations…boundaries set for us. We are given only so much latitude in opening our minds to what is possible. And although we are told that anything is possible, we are fed the opposite. This includes our scientists as well. Boundaries are set in our minds about the manner in which reality functions as well as limitations about our individual abilities, our function and our impact on the process of EXPERIENCING!

Quantum physics and science in general presents us with small insights into the mechanics of cosmic technology. But our tendency is to limit this technology to scientific findings. The technology of energy is much too vast and it responds according to the intelligence rubbing the genie's lamp. It is responding according to the magnitude of the consciousness, or the creative force behind the action or thought.

What is it that we fear in being exposed to the unlimited or to the unknown? Are we challenged in stretching our minds beyond current perceptions and conclusions fed to us about the nature of reality? It is necessary to ask these questions…it allows us to determine if our objections are supported by anything worth holding on to.

To recognize that the universe as understood is simply a system within which a particular kind of experience, or reality construct is taking place is freeing. It is not a conclusive space but rather an echo descending from an endless space. The human experience which we are engaged in is a component of this universe's system design. All planets exist in response to the protocols of this particular universal system. It is why the element of time is so significant to us."

Quote was taken from my

(Sonia Barrett - www.spiritinform.com) lecture in 2011- Decoding the Matrix of Time, Reality and Cycles.

These characters are significant in the universal design. They are attached to the holographic recorder keeper called the soul. It is how characters live on through karmic debts. Characters are more of a straw-man or robot. These idea patterns are continuously morphing as new ideas are formed. Although the life of the character is embedded in the story, we must seek to evolve the roles being played and reintegrate them in the more profound version of who we truly are. These idea patterns ultimately emerge from us. Through these characters and these bodies we become the imagined. We become the dream.

"Viewing the raw constructs of the human experience is necessary for those who are ready to peer more deeply behind the curtain of paradox. This kind of readiness emerges when we are free to be unlimited. Although many express the idea of being unlimited this is most often pursued with restrictive views on reality. The idea of being unlimited by personal definition would mean that there is a desire to explore potentials beyond the illusionary restrictions of physical reality. It is a realization that the very laws of physics are a construct or boundaries set within our own minds. The stuff of life by which your construct of reality is formed then responds to those boundaries and limitations that your mind is plugged into. Many of our limitations and preconceived notions about the nature of existence go back to our parents and the external managing systems we encounter as we embark on this life's journey. When we enter this life, most of us bring with us old concepts and old beliefs, old limitations, old bloodline beliefs, old ancestral boundaries, old fear, and so on. It is clear that we do arrive with a set of baggage and the conditions we choose in embarking on this life supports those roles and the direction that one will shift into or maintain throughout the journey. However, it is within our power to create new holograms."

Quote taken from (Sonia Barrett-www.spiritinform.com) lecture in 2011- Decoding the Matrix of Time, Reality and Cycles.

In removing the shackles of the game, we must recognize the limitations that we continue to defend. What confirmations do we have that life must be lived under the protocols that we have been exposed to perhaps all our lives. We often speak of God but it is necessary to reevaluate your reference. Who or what are you speaking of? The game is devised of endless layers of mind mazes. By whose rules are we playing? Are there any absolutes in deciphering reality? Absolutes are comfort zones. It provides us with a sense of control. Who is it that needs to feel in control …perhaps the character or robot. Losing control is a gift. This kind of control is artificial and serves to secure our illusions. The shackles have become a security blanket, for it shields us from letting go of old concepts and beliefs. It assures us a life of continued limiting idea patterns. We are shackled by the fear of discovering that we are not what we thought we were. Somehow we fear a decrease in our value individually and collectively. This is a slave mentality.

We worry about borders and immigration issues, and health care issues, and political candidates, and spiritual concepts that promise the ideal afterlife. Give us anything but freedom! This is indeed the nature of the game; no right or wrong however. There is a high price for freedom. Freedom means self-reliance, freedom is about mastering the game; freedom is about letting go of comfort zones and not "going gently into that good night without a fight", poet Dylan

Thomas. The game is about the beginning and the ending of cycles and themes. What we truly are supersedes these cycles and themes. Cycles and themes are protocols for the regulation of collective consciousness. They establish boundaries and guidelines in the human game. They determine the concept of *time*!

Whatever your story entails at this moment; stop and decode it, for there lays the answer to the changes you seek to make in your life. You are not bound by the apparent protocols of reality, but you are rather a free agent (we each know if this is true for us). One may choose to release or to remain committed to these boundaries. No one loses, for we are always where we choose to be. So where do you choose to be? There lies the treasure in your response. The answers are always there.

5

Government, Religion, and Education; Keepers of the Matrix Part 1
Subtle running programs of self-imprisonment

It is evident that there is a collective concept or interpretation of reality that is shared by many. (To even use the word *many* is speculative because it is not understood quantitatively who is experiencing what. It is simply a general assumption that the world and reality can even be quantitatively verified.) Reality is loosely defined; it is taking place in a field of frequencies supporting particular optical, audio, and textural patterns. These are patterns that everyone around us appears to respond to. These patterns are specific to our five base senses. The system also supports a network of human emotions according to the protocols of this reality. Although our sensory capability exceeds five senses, these five senses establish a centralized point of connection for interplay. So in essence, there is a general operating program in place for the manner in which we function as human beings (reference to humans based on the current perception of reality) and how we will evolve collectively within this hologram. The system is structured to support collective evolution. Individualized progression is more of an override to the system.

Within the hologram are programs supporting order and control. Such programs are run through familiar systems of government, religion, and education. Despite the seeming uniqueness in our lives, unless one is removed from the general dependency encouraged by these systems, then one is subject to the protocols in place for the collective experience. Reality is such a cleverly functioning experience that one can spend much time chasing after self-awareness, yet remain caught in just another one of the many system designed awareness matrix. In examining the governmental system in the region, one may reside the dependency of people on government as their protector, which is a familiar tale worldwide. Conditions are created in order to ensure the need of government. Self-examination might also bring to the surface subtle degrees of that program. Where did much of this kind of belief system emerge from? This is not to say that we should disband the idea of government, but we should examine the manner in which we have surrendered personal charge over our own lives. An observation of the immediate reality around us would confirm that most people are not ready to take responsibility; proving government essential.

When people have been programmed to be compliant, the decision making process in their lives are easily transferred to the overseers. Humanity has been *trained* to take orders; this includes even those that lead. This is the purpose of modern day education. It is indeed true that education was not always this way, but even then the programming existed side by side in subtle ways. A trail of the execution of such programs can be seen in the stories of space visitors and in mythical stories of gods and supernatural forces, impressing humanity with belief systems of inferiority and fear. In essence, the human race (as currently experienced) has been disconnected from the truth of its potentials for such a long time, that even those who write and speak about the atrocities of government, education, and religion are unable to see their own imprisonment in an even greater deception.

One may acknowledge that we have been deceived, and in the same breath defend limiting religious and spiritual beliefs. Such beings remain oblivious to their own programs. Should their beliefs be examined, perhaps the holes in these beliefs would be made evident, yet they may continue to remain committed to such concepts. Belief systems are powerfully strong, as it is the method by which the technology of the body operates. The human experience is based on automatic programs which, in translation, are programmed beliefs. This has been a programmed experience engineered in a way that has provided an assortment of concepts from which we extract our choices. This act of choosing personalizes our decision and further authorizes a sense of freedom which ultimately is a deceptive picture of freedom. This becomes our reference point of being free, while all along there is very little authentic choice. This same game is played by government, religion, and education.

The concept of going within has been infiltrated in so many ways that the simplicity of engaging in such a natural experience now requires third parties to create this connection for us. This is much like the days of dialing the long distance operator to establish connection. It is interesting to note that zero (0) is the number of choice in dialing the operator! How interesting is that? Connecting with the operator links us with a voice somewhere out there. Zero point (0.), that's the space we aim for in meditation. Zero point (0.) is the no-spin zone, or immeasurable spin, where time is seemingly nonexistent. The fluctuation between a wave and a particle is then evident. This is a powerful space of creating. Such an occurrence expresses the lowest energy state of a particle field, also known as its ground field state. In referencing the electromagnetic spectrum we can view zero point (0.) as the apex. All fields descend from this space and each frequency progressively enfolds one in the other on the way up; Radio wave, infrared, invisible light, ultraviolet light, x-ray, Gamma Ray, and so on, as the acceleration of the spin (the frequency) increases.

Within us is the fabric of creation. When we close our eyes a magnificent moment occurs, there is nothing and we are then free to imagine a different version of reality, be it qualified as real or unreal. Each time that we close our eyes we experience the canvas upon which our imagination paints. Our conditioning for survival is fed by the systems in place, diverting us to other structured concepts and beliefs. Our base survival program is for food, clothes, and shelter; however, this has gradually progressed to a different level of survival. They would become barometers for identity and classification. Our obsession with personal beauty, the kinds of clothes we wear, both the location and kind of dwelling we occupy, has now thrown a smokescreen over the core survival program. The game in reference to this core program is so variegated that we find ourselves either running from being part of these social classifications or running toward it. Very seldom do we stand on a middle ground.

Everything is either good or bad for us. We are either committed to being spiritual and financially impoverished, as this seems to be a qualifying ideal for spiritual humility; which is yet another program. Alongside such misconceptions are spiritual leaders spreading exaggerated notions about financial abundance while corporatizing spirituality. Spirituality is about the free flow of current in all areas of one's life as essential to one's journey. Currency, aka money, should not be associated with guilt or deprivation in attaining enlightenment. This is a program which suppresses our ownership of being creators. Poverty or lack supports a belief system of non-equality to those who seem to possess the skill or the art of creative flow. This is a program rooted in the system's design, allowing the polarized experience of being on either side of the coin. However, one may switch sides not simply through attending hundreds of abundance workshops but by understanding that the core belief/program/imprint must be changed, followed by actual change.

Although financial success may have already been achieved if one hoards their money, has fear of spending it, if one is simply content with seeing the numbers in one's account, or has fear of ever returning to an experience of lack these are all signs that those core program still exists. If your life hinges on the credit bureaus, and the life of your 401k, then you have placed yourself as creator on hold in the bigger picture. What you have done is commit the flow of your life to the finite conditions of the matrix program. Remember that the system is automated. This does not mean that we should not take care of our credit and 401k, but more importantly understand that you are playing a game, that's what the credit bureau is, that's what your 401k is, just like the stock market. You must play life for the fun of it...this is a shocking thought to some, but that is the magic of it all. We must play life for fun because it is not this finite experience that our minds are so locked into believing, or as the system would have us believe. We must examine our attitude and thought process in the way in which we experience money. This money program seems to be one of the most challenging experiences for many. Friends and family are torn apart by this psychological experience called money.

This polarized process of being rich or poor, good or bad, are cousins to each other. Combinations are mixed and matched like a potion resulting in the manner in which we pursue our survival cures. How we establish food, clothes, and shelter then range from simple to complex, especially when the emotions of power and control are thrown in the mix. One is then affected by the overseeing forces influencing his or her survival strategies. This involves government, corporations, education, and spiritual or religious practices. The life force, or blood, for such systems is the fuel of power and control. This is not a good or bad thing, for without individuals holding such programs, there would be no leaders in a reality where one's journey may be about experiencing submission and in being controlled. What do you choose to experience? What have you been experiencing? Cursing the rich only serves to uphold your own programs. Money has been made the enemy, upheld by a very contradictory mindset. We expect to receive, yet we curse the energy. The governing force of the collective currency experiences on the planet understands our schizophrenic relationship with money, and so we are pupated by pitting the poor against the wealthy and the wealthy against the poor. There are two distinct classes divided, yet they are both robots and pawns in the game. This creates such distractions that we seem to be permanently cast in the roles of victim and victimizer, rich and poor, which most often becomes generational.

We focus on suggested beliefs about the economy; is it a good economy or bad economy? The uncertainty of our jobs are no longer secure…but were they ever? Perhaps this was all in your head. If your name does not appear on your employer's bank account then security was always an illusion. If you run a business, there is always an opportunity to alter it, close it, or convert it to something you have always wanted to try your mind at. To buy into the economy is to do just that...buy into you; you purchase the idea with emotional dollars and this begins to confirm the state of the economy in your reality. We further find others to support just how bad it is. The fact is that there are people with an overabundance of money who are ready to secure your services, whatever that may be; but if the energy you project is of the economy being bad, then no one will buy, and the universe must comply with your wishes. You shall surely receive potential customers who complain that they would love to have your service if only they had the money, but that the economy is bad. Instead, establish a belief that expects those able to afford your services to show up.

The awareness that we create our reality is replaced by these characters we play, and the scripts we read from. In the meanwhile, the wheel of the greater matrix continues to turn and churn out programs for the unsuspecting groups who will live and die according to these programs. We hear of brain plasticity:

1-"Brain plasticity refers to the capacity of the nervous system to change its structure and its function over a lifetime, in reaction to environmental diversity. Although this term is now commonly used in psychology and neuroscience, it is not easily defined and is used to refer to changes at many levels in the nervous system ranging from molecular events, such as changes in gene expression, to behavior."

To take a true examination of one's life is the key. Moving toward making the desired changes is the next greatest key. There is plasticity in our design therefore change is a plausible action. Change is not about blame, guilt, or regret it is about experiencing greater levels of consciousness. Commit to your own evolution, it is the gateway beyond an automated life.

6

Government, Religion, and Education: Keepers of the Matrix Part 2
Reality – a Result of the Vibration of Collective and Individual Consciousness

To understand that such systems are instrumental in holding the game in place, is to understand the necessity of those roles they play. These systems are running programs. They act as pilots of the survival program. We are reminded that the game is about survival...or so we are lead to believe. Planetary life reflects the adage of "survival of the fittest". What is to be contemplated is that this virtual life is about the experiencing of everything. The survival program seems to induce evolution upon us as a species and as individuals. The entire cosmic experience is about possibilities. How those possibilities unfold is unique to the individual.

We are wired for different kinds of experiences according to our bloodline, ancestral line, and the requirements of the journey. Life is being experienced not by random acts, but by a series of conditions that are aligned in order to achieve the mission of the journey. For some, the journey is about awakening to the cosmic game from a level requiring no go-betweens, but instead complete ownership of one's self as creator; others will require a go-between along with fantastic stories causing distractions from owning personal power; another's journey might involve being completely submerged in the earthly experience with no desire to be awakened on any level.

Although 2012 is viewed as bringing a complete consciousness overhaul, there are different interpretations of what that overhaul entails. It is important to remain open to the fact there are a number of misinterpretations of ancient history along the lines of planetary evolution. It is essential that we consider the possibility of an evolutionary leap from times past that were really about a vibrational leap. This, of course, still entails a shift in consciousness. This kind of potential shift more than likely would involve a pocket or handful of people not necessarily bound together as a singular group mind. This kind of leap, more than likely, is undocumented or misinterpreted as the common human perception, generally leaning toward planetary destruction and annihilation of the human race.

Such a leap would appear to be a shift into an invisible space just a shade above this (assuming we are sharing a common view) reality. It is then invisible to participants of a lower vibrating consciousness or reality. The point is that reality exists in vibrational layers. It would also be a natural progression for the individual, just as we journey from one country to the next, or from one town to the next. Why? Because the individual has been progressively moving through the necessary changes and shifts beyond the automated programs and cycles. We are only seeing what we are immediately focused on. Standing in this space of awareness further opens our minds and brings latitude to our perception in stepping beyond group or collective limitations. This is not about expelling energy in figuring out whether we are shifting into the fifth or sixth dimension. This is about fluidly progressing as we become more of who we really are. Such concepts are safety nets for us, because as human beings the idea of wandering into the unknown is terrifying. Although we might not be familiar with the fifth or sixth dimension, there is a sense of comfort in having the name of a location in mind. We are seeking security and assuredness.

The science or design of the playground of consciousness cannot be limited to finite paradigms. Consciousness constructs reality according to awareness of the individual, or of the collective. Individuals operating in a more expansive state of awareness have the opportunity to move between worlds. Does this sound farfetched? It is not farfetched when viewed as profound science. We are experiencing the shape shifting of energy. What limits us, are our perceptual boundaries.

"The Explicate Order, weakest of all energy systems, resonates out of and is an expression of an internal infinitely more powerful order of energy called the Implicate order. It is the precursor of the Explicate, the internal dreamlike vision or the ideal presentation of that which is to become manifest as a physical object. The Implicate order implies within it all physical universes. However, it resonates from an energy field which is yet greater, the realm of pure potential. It is pure potential because nothing is implied within it; implications form in the implicate order and then express themselves in the explicate order. Bohm goes on to postulate a final state of internal infinite [zero point] energy which he calls the realm of insight intelligence. The creative internal process springs from this realm. Energy is generated there, gathers its pure potential, and implies within its eventual expression as the explicate order." Will Keepin, David Bohm, Noetic Science Journal

Scientists like David Bohm give rise to the possibility of these closely layered realms. In the above quote he speaks of the realm of pure potential; *"It is pure potential because nothing is implied within it"* he goes on further to say that *"implications form in the implicate order and then express themselves in the explicate order"*. This becomes significant when we consider that all forms of reality are observer-based and shows itself according to the perception, or the consciousness, of the participant. We become engaged with a version of reality relevant to our own progression. It is here that we can see how and why *"implications form in the implicate order and then express themselves in the explicate order."*

To further address the idea of these invisible realms is to understand the wave particle phenomenon. We are referencing Non-locality where a wave is sharing the same Non-space as a particle; so in other words a wave doesn't suddenly become a particle it already is. This defines the interconnectedness of all life, one not separate from the other. However, what establishes this sense of distinction is the manner in which the observer impacts the field. Reality is embedded in a multi-highway of realms in the same manner as the particle wave function. Nevertheless, our allegiance is singularly directed, allowing the illusion of a single realm of existence. We are operating on multiple streams despite the apparent single experience.

In establishing relevance for these systems in place, it is significant to view them as spokes in a wheel. They maintain movement in a particular way according to the needs of the participants of the experience. They work along the lines of order and control on levels requiring these protocols. Without properly examining the process, we are left confused about the apparent state of the world, along with the personal challenges we face. We question the necessity of these experiences and hope for an ending to this conflict filled reality.

The mind is endless, limited only by the guided and guarded experiences in this concept of reality. Is the mind actually an aspect of space, although a hologram with signatures specific to the individual? Although the potential exists for expansive perceptions and thoughts, a collective agreement remains in place; certifying a synchronized concept of reality. This limits latitude in the collective human experience unless regulated by the progression of stages in place, known as evolution. The mind then operates in a regulated manner resulting in a narrow perception base. Therefore, all systems of restrictions are part of the protocols specific to the kind of collective experience being addressed here.

Reality is then synonymous to the wave particle movement. All things physical, including our bodies, exist as a result of this wave particle dance. This wave particle performance is responding to mind, perceptions, and thoughts, and collectively they are the sum total of the vibration of our consciousness. We are then greeted by reality according to this calculation; the frequency output of collective consciousness or individualized consciousness. The state of the world is a result of this formula.

There is a feedback loop in action, as we are both transmitters and receivers. There is an exchange of information that is being carried out across a vast network. Neurons firing beliefs and probabilities once they get the green light.

> "The brain operates off of electrical signals in the form of an image. Sensory stimuli are processed in the brain as a stream of electrical impulses created by neurons firing. Neurons are a group of cells specializing in specific functions such as the assembly of blood, organs, glands, bones etc. The body is comprised of billions of cells, which categorically form the entire organism; however, the brain includes billions of neurons, which begin "firing" messages upon stimuli of the five senses. These messages are in the form of hormones, chemicals, and electrical impulses." Excerpt from The Holographic Canvas by Sonia Barrett

The fact that neurons fire even before the evidence of a selected choice does not mean that there is no free will. It would imply that a conclusive choice or thought emerges from the abyss, or the core of probabilities, before a conscious thought is formed. The choice was known in waver form and beyond. The choice was simply one existing in the stream of probabilities and potentials.

In the Princeton Engineering Anomalies Research (PEAR) they have been able to conclude through research that the influence of human consciousness on a global level generates less than random results. These experiments were conducted to determine the effects of major global events on collective consciousness. The experiments involved such events as: after the death of Diana, Princess of Wales in September 1997, as well as the events of 9/11. This is similar to the rapid dispersion of signals (information) throughout the brain when neurons fire. Further comparison was made stating that "the rapid dispersion of such a signal mimics the spread of ideas and behaviors in social networks; a sufficiently provocative idea can spread very swiftly through a population."

What this statement confirms is the collective agreement held in place regarding the current model of reality. We can each act as a neuron firing with new insights and new models of reality. The diversity and complexity of how we exist collectively or individually in creating our own reality can be perplexing. However, as we establish the model of reality ideal for us, there will be base concepts of commonality with other players. Perhaps all the players or characters are really you! With that being said, it stands to reason that each of us should focus on internal changes and in widening our perception as this will open doors to the untapped field of potentials. To speculate from a perception of impossibility will only ensure a reality limited by ones perceptions. Is it possible that in an alternate reality we are each living the life we dream of? It's quite possible for if indeed reality is all smoke and mirrors, and that wave and particle are one in the same waiting to embark on the next potential based on the observer, then self-progression is the key! Not group or Borg like philosophies, unless one particularly chooses that experience. We should also keep in mind that in a hologram, any part of that hologram contains the whole. So as individuals, we represent various potentials of the whole; we are the whole; as this is a holographic experience.

Reshaping one's reality requires experiencing new ideas, thoughts, and beliefs. The brain compiles all new information emerging from new experiences and forms new thoughts. This, in turn, creates new interference patterns as new content is added to the library of the brain. Widening one's perception allows new experiences and probabilities which present a fluctuation in interference patterns, a necessity in creating new models of reality. We are then establishing our own personal evolution.

GOVERNMENT, RELIGION, CORPORATIONS, AND EDUCATION; KEEPERS OF THE MATRIX, these systems keep us focused on external solutions. Most all our restrictive programs arrive via these systems. Social coding and value systems are established under these organizations. In turn, the stories we create, our beliefs, and the manner in which we define ourselves are generated from these systems. (For those living outside of modern day civilization they are still part of the collective consciousness network and so there are base limiting concepts that we share as a collective.) These systems in place are organized organisms having a life of their own, fueled by the emotions and minds of people. What is important to remember is the core design of the system which supports evolution according to regulated cycles. The year 2012 is seen as a period initiating an upsurge in collective consciousness. This is based on a cyclic timer.

The fact is that we are each responsible for our own personal progression, not necessarily based on time frames as orchestrated by the astrological schedule for evolution. To release blame or anger with the systems in place is to certify one understands that those are tools of the automated reality. They serve their purpose, for not all of humanity is clamoring for profound introspection and deep cosmic insight. The system is therefore responding to the majority of collective consciousness. Very few become invisible to this automated system, but those that have may very well walk among us with an awareness of those who are on their way to crossing that threshold. These are beings crossing over not from an understanding of fear, or of escape, but in an appreciation of every moment in the human experience. There is no longer a polarized view of reality as good or bad, but instead they embrace a realization of the smoke and mirror of the human experience. There is then a true readiness to experience a more unlimited reality! Every moment is truly a rich experience as we move about in an ocean of unlimited potentials. This journey continues to take us into forever, for that's what we already are...Forever!

7

Life Beyond the Programs of 2012

Based on our methods of mapping time, every twelve months we enter a new phase on the cyclic wheel. Our consciousness then shifts and occupies this new time cycle. It is viewed as an opportunity to recycle ourselves or a starting over point with new resolutions. However, this is met with great contradictions as we interact with these cycles like a game of Russian roulette; no one knows when their number will be up. Concepts and ideas about each new cycle are established for us by others such as religion, government, and education channeled through various mediums. We solidify and seal these conclusions by historical data presented to us by trusted sources. Whether these sources are trusted or not does not necessarily establish what we will accept as a belief, for we are influenced by the greater social network which forms the overall collective experience.

There are a few base beliefs and agreements in regards to the mechanics of the general cosmic cycles. We then establish a footing on those general beliefs and proceed with constructing our individual models of reality. The cycle of 2012 has a great many interpretations associated with it. There is, however, a collective acceptance that it is the ending of a cycle and for some it means the end of the world, and for others it means an ending and a beginning. The fact is that for some the world will end as they have been experiencing it in a body, these are people who have expired before entering the new cycle of 2012. What we believe and what we desire at the core of our subconscious shapes the journey and the outcome. Whether we assume an atheistic approach or one of a Supreme Being guiding humanity through these changes still does not break the vulnerability felt towards this automated cycling through of life. We debate over whether our lives are random or driven by choice. Much of the evidence of the mechanics of this moving carnival can be seen throughout the voyage of our journey. We can clearly see the rippling effect of the choices we have made.

In order to move beyond this sense of vulnerability, one must question the possibility that life as viewed and experienced is limited to a one-dimensional view of human life on earth. If indeed we are prepped with ideas and concepts about each new cycle to follow, then is it possible that such projections have overshadowed other less limiting concepts of reality? However, we hold firmly to reaffirming the collective limitations. Many find it comforting to know that others support the same base model of reality. We are challenged when our beliefs about the nature of reality stands alone. Many are overwhelmed with the notion of ascension and concerned with who makes it and who doesn't. Many are still unclear about what this shift is supposed to mean. They speak of making the shift, but making it to where? There is this sense that suddenly the wars will stop, everyone will be in love with each other, and we will emerge as our magical self, and that could very well be the case for some. The fact is that the individual has always had the opportunity to experience such things. However, this *head in the sand* concept of ascension creates this free ride scenario as we are whisked off to this magical place. For many, this is more about escaping the chaos of the world. Our relationship with the world around us is dependent on our beliefs, needs, and ultimately our story. So escaping our perception of the world is very different than changing our perception of the world. Such changes can only occur when we acknowledge the limitations of our beliefs and recognize that our desire to escape rests on a foundation of fear.

The ultimate concept of ascension is about ascending into a more expansive expression of ourselves as creators. It is about falling in love with the magic of reality just as it is. Why is that? Because when we are in this space of understanding that life is no longer viewed as good or bad, right or wrong, but more from an understanding that each being is playing and experiencing reality according to his or her own perception of reality.

Maybe it's simply not a preferred experience, or something else is preferred?

"Since everything is but an apparition
Perfect in being what it is
Having nothing to do with good or bad
Acceptance or rejection
One may well burst out in laughter"
Tibetan Buddhist, Longehenpa

Babies preselect the ideal environment for their experience on this journey. Although, it is a rather challenging thought, it makes little sense to place the responsibility of having made that choice on the adult version of the child. It would stand to reason when examining the course of our journey from conception onward, we will recognize that the dots connect in bringing us to this very moment in time. We can clearly see the chain of events that have interlinked in leading us through the journey of our lives. We are ultimately ascending into a more expansive playing field variationally but this is an individual process. To align with such an understanding does not mean that our emotional expressions become limited to a masked display of joy, but rather we allow all emotions to move through without judgment. We embrace it all, as love is not a conditional experience or force, but instead it encompasses all potentials and possibilities. Love is an expression of *"allowing"*.

Adverse experiences are perhaps more the result of imposed limitations based on belief systems and programs. This makes us ripe for any concept that promises to deliver us from the tape playing in our own heads. In an attempt to purge those programs and beliefs which have been directing our lives every action, thought, choice, and experience shows us the running programs. Most often we do not recognize it as such, and instead we form conclusions that keep us enslaved and victims of our lives. Yet all along, that which holds us hostage is also showing us the way. The magnificence and intelligence of the spirit is made invisible in order to validate our victimization and helplessness. In such a process, we will either seek to save the world and punish our victimizers, or we can gift the world by seeing through the fog of our own blockages.

> *"Though one should conquer a thousand times a thousand men in battle, he who conquers his own self, is the greatest of all conquerors. Self-conquest is, indeed, far greater than the conquest of all other folks."* Dhammapada v. 103, 104

It is very clear that we cannot save the world, for the world does not need saving, it is the individual who holds a responsibility to his or herself in recoding their life. Setting out to save the world has adverse effects, yet a necessary one for both parties; the one who is being saved and the one doing the saving. The feeling of saving others fills us with purpose and serves as a distraction from our own hidden beliefs that lead us to the idea of saving the world in the first place. Our actions are not random, neither are our thoughts. How we see the world only serves to create more of the same thing. We can certainly choose to experience the world differently, but our assessment of the world and our reasons for wishing for this change makes a difference in how it all unfolds. To understand reality as a game becomes a major tool in transforming our model of reality. When we view the players and the game of reality as an enemy, we continue to be its energy source. It takes a tremendous amount of energy to hold all of our dislikes in place. It requires focus and diligence, which we do with ease as this is a familiar mode of operation. Collectively, we continue to hold the same old model in place, and when we attempt to replace it with something else, we do so from the perspective of good or bad. The good and bad concept is a conflict code. Aiming to operate from a perspective of resonance directs the energy to the creation of a new game or playing field. Energy is then not being drained in support of our dislike for the old model.

Every moment is a grand opportunity to awaken to our necessary personal changes. We are always in the midst of opportunities for personal evolution. While feeling challenged by adversities we can examine each circumstance, and perhaps trace the events and thought processes that has led to this moment. What exactly do you want? What did you ask for? What did you wish for time and time again? Perhaps this is the route that it will take to get you there. Nothing is as it seems however the longer we sit lamenting and feeling sorry for ourselves, the longer it will take for us to move into that new solution. The landlord, the bank, the utility company, the finance company, the friend, the enemy, the spouse, the mate, the child, the relative, the employer, the health crisis...what are they all gifting you with? Seeing the gift is the challenge because there is pain and aloneness, confusion and uncertainties. Reading the Data Stream of Reality (Sonia's workshop) speaks about reading the data in everything. This is about reading life like a computer printout. It is all showing you something, but in order to read the data, one must step away from the emotions of judgment and simply observe. Transcending the process of blaming others will speed up the process of reading or seeing the gift. Seeing the potential gift grants permission for the conditions to shift. The conditions shift much slower when we are stabilizing these particles in support of our emotions.

Since we create our own reality, frequency patterns and particles stabilize to form our reality according to our beliefs and perceptions about our lives. This is a science which we embrace selectively according to less complicated moments in our lives. The fact is that every moment of our life is constructed in this manner. Again, positive thinking and mantras don't work when our core belief programs do not support such thinking. So we keep repeating the same cycles. The year 2012, like all preceding cycles comes with its own codes and programs for the unfolding of human life in this new cycle. Remember that many are coded to participate in this 2012 cyclic program and will be here through the full cycle. We have been primed for the energies of 2012 which will implement or trigger new levels of coding within humans, preparing them for the next step in both cosmic and earthly technology integration. This should not be seen as the unleashing of victimization but from a perspective of an awakened, being that is now aware of the systems protocols. Here such awakened beings have an opportunity to ride those same frequencies in establishing one's own inner activation beyond the limitations of the 2012 program.

Those who are in that space of thought will see through what is being said here and step beyond the fantastic tales that have been told to humanity for eons. If this is indeed understood then one will not spend focus waiting for 12/12/12 or 11/11 of any format, these are codes and triggers. Reality is all about numbers; this is a math game; quantum packets of energy shaping reality. All things possess a numerical value; it's all energy. We respond to numbers because of the numeric structure of our world, from the sky to the earth and everything in-between. This is like a coloring book with numbers directing you to the color to be used. We operate in a specific set of numerical coding which our brain is well aware of, and so it would not be difficult to use numbers as triggers for certain kinds of activation and brain wave re-patterning. According to the special theory of relativity, reality is four-dimensional, time being the fourth dimension. This is a four-dimensional space-time continuum where past, present, and future ultimately exists all at the same time. Reality as experienced is happening in a mathematically formulated space which specifically supports the kind of experience that we, as humans, are wired for. This formula is further supported, or held together, by these cycles. It is possible for us to move outside of that space.

The year 2012 is yet another component in this cosmic wheel, here to guide us through until we awaken to greater truths about who we are and the extent of our capabilities. There are those whose entire reality is dependent on the predictions of 2012. How we perceive these new cycles for ourselves as individuals will determine exactly how we will experience this new phase. Embrace life and play it like a game. Energy spent focusing on what we believe was done to us can be converted into fuel, to propel us to greater levels of understanding. Such levels propel us into more expansive stages of consciousness which ultimately begins to override realities supported by a less expansive consciousness. We can then tap into the magic of creating new holograms. Some might say that this is easier said than done, but to spend time hiding behind the fear of reaching for that possibility will only position us back in the same space on January 1, 2013.

> *"If I am right in saying that thought is the ultimate origin or source, it follows that if we don't do anything about thought, we won't get anywhere. We may momentarily relieve the population problem, the ecological problem, and so on, but they will come back in another way."* D. Bohm & Mark Edwards, Changing Consciousness

It is vital to remember that one's life as experienced in this very moment is only as real as we allow it to be. Remember that *real* is the realm of focus. How we interpret this moment's experience determines the shape, color, and texture of our personal reality. What we focus on establishes the playing field, and the ground rules, for the manner in which we choose to play. It further determines the characters and the events that will appear to support the conclusions established in our minds about the nature of our life and the immediate world around us. According to Quantum mechanics, particles can also behave as waves fluctuating and moving into a direction or form based on the observer; this is a reminder that observation takes place through the perception filter of the observer. If there are beliefs, concepts, and people that you need to release, then let them go so that your story may be different. These conditions and people are there as a result of our model of reality. Although 2012 is yet another cycle of programs view it as an opportunity to become more than the predictions. You are the reason for every star that hangs in the sky. You are the field on which you play!

8

Cyclic Engineering: Going Offline in the Game

Have you looked in the mirror lately? Is there an age progression occurring? Have you ever stopped to ask yourself why? Chances are that you have accepted this as a natural process, just as most everyone has. Have you for a moment thought that perhaps there is foul play at work, or that there might possibly be an alternative to this deterioration, other than the next likely option of death? What if the game is at your expense? This entire process is so accepted and defended. This is an amazing game of deception of immeasurable magnitude. There is a difference between deterioration and getting older.

To exist endlessly through the cycles of time is very different than the vibrational deterioration of the physical body. This physical deterioration process is a result of being on the grid, or being online, in this engineered time construct. Look around you for models of the very system that holds your life in position on the grid; such things as smart grid ties power sources in, and around, our homes and cities to one linkage point. This communication network has similarities to that of the internet. It's like establishing a portal of open communication which can then create interceptions and adjustments from key linkage points. These are mini replicas of the outer matrix which enfolds the smaller matrix we call reality.

Both these systems create links between our minds and our emotional fields, much of which is done through these convenient technologies that are now largely a part of our daily lives. We are part of a wireless network specifically relating to the matrix of these *"time" cycles;* cycles are time related for they quantify space. We are all online, on network systems within the game. This is not a good or bad thing its simply part of the game. You may not choose to live beyond the general number of years, and that's ok, but perhaps if given a choice, one would prefer to experience life in a more youthful manner. Epigenetics research now confirms that it is our perceptions and beliefs that determine the changes which take place in the body; much of this information is now shared by Dr. Bruce Lipton. Although science may now incorporate this as a new found realization, there are still boundaries placed on the outrageous possibilities that can emerge in the body based on an expansive perception. We must begin to stretch our imagination!

When we are unaware of the bigger picture, it allows full submersion, whereby having the fullest experience. When we go to our place of employment we create our own game within the already designed game field of the employer. So, it is in this game of cycles experienced as reality or life. We accept the cycling through of segments, of time allotted for our lives; but by whose design? That is the question. Is there a core game designer for this particular game experience? Is this the ultimate God or Creator that we somehow seek to connect with? Our thoughts and beliefs seem to be automatically wired to support these base assertions. The idea of living outside of this grid of thought is unsettling for most, followed by defensive responses such as; we can't live forever, or that all things die because that's the way it is.

There are a myriad of excuses executed by the mind, regardless of religious or spiritual beliefs; somehow the core programs about life and death ultimately win out as the overriding conclusion. To know that nothing dies, for everything is made up of energy, creates a level of comfort, as we anticipate an unavoidable encounter with death. Even within the most spiritually advanced practices; those incorporating scientific discoveries; they too are overpowered by the imprisoning programs of life and death. We are programmed to accept that this is the only way. After all life, as it is played out around us, seems to support and confirms that this is the only way. No one wants to set themselves up for disappointment by going against the grain. But what if none of this is set in stone? Even those who consider themselves "awakened" seem to encounter the same pitfall. There is much talk about the illusion of time and life, yet in the same breath death becomes a welcomed transition. Validations, such as mentioned previously, are used to support this kind of thinking. Certainly, reincarnation is viewed as an opportunity to recycle (read the book The Holographic Canvas). This adds comfort. Could there be deception in the reincarnation loop? What if our minds are simply caught in a space/position in time or perhaps no time that is simply a projection, held in place by programs relevant and essential to our confinement. Although consciousness has free reign the vehicle of consciousness, it is evidently subject to these projections within that realm of space time.

There seems to be some sort of block that does not allow most of us to entertain thoughts reaching outside of the boundaries of these collective beliefs. Like everything else, your thoughts are frequency patterns; those frequency patterns generally remain within the realm of the (belief) frequency established in the core system. (I don't want to live that long; what am I going to do with that much time? what would I even do?; why would I want to outlive everyone I know?). What limiting beliefs! Not for one moment can you imagine that this life, as you have been living, it is not the ultimate in possibilities. What if life as you evolve in awareness is reshaped? What if such an evolution shifts not only your consciousness but your physical body to a more expansive realm of time? What if, as you penetrate these boundaries of time, you meet others who have also crossed the bridge of linear time?

We have heard many stories about the Annunaki and other beings that have played a role in human evolution. There is much talk about genetic engineering. It is indeed evident that there are suppressed abilities and possibilities for this human body. In much of the history presented in reference to such beings, a common thread has been the fact that they were able to live for hundreds of thousands of years. Humans, however, were engineered to live much shorter life spans for reasons of population control, perhaps to ensure shorter knowledge spans. It is said that those who were direct descendants, maintained the coding of these beings and were able to live longer lives (hence we have elite groups on the planet who view themselves as superior or who seek to maintain pure bloodlines). However, there is one core ingredient that overrides even the highest level of engineering and that would be the consciousness that is the true owner of the vessel. It is also common practice to speak about the significance of the soul which is generally revered or approached from a place of mysticism.

The soul is a holographic record keeper that keeps track of the travels of consciousness or more specifically the journey of the lower vibration of itself (or self) as experienced and expressed through the body. With that being said, we must understand that the body has been redirected to take orders from the subconscious mind and to only function by way of the programs in the subconscious. This automated self is designed to override anything that is not run through the subconscious mind. As part of the navigation process, the body is networked into these cycles. A full-fledged robotic, automated system was now in place. The cycles would keep the body online based on the programs of this reality or realm. There are three different phases of being online (1) there is the general birth to death online program (2) there is being online but overriding the general program (3), option 2 can also be viewed as going offline--free flowing through, above and beyond the systems standard protocol. We can go offline from the limiting matrix program and go online with the core system, where there are no limitations established by the system once certain levels of decoding have taken place within us.

Technically, 2012 represents a rebooting of the system, an evolution to the game. It is the end of a 104,000 year theme and the beginning of an upgrade to the game of cycles. There is a tremendous amount of squabble over the correct dates; incorrect calendars. What we must keep in mind is that all calendars simply mark the cycles in this particular system. Calendars keep track of the linear time cycles by and through, which is how the game functions. Jose Arguelles talks about the original calendar, but that too is a game regulator. It might, however, assist in your move out of the familiar oppressive frequency of the Gregorian calendar, but keep in mind that all calendars support the robotic self. Each day represents specific frequencies supporting the unique experiences we each have according to our individual reality program. Even prior to the creation of any known form of the calendar, humans were still tied into some sort of calculative time construct for the cycling through of their daily lives. The calculation of time gradually became more significant in the counting down of years as it influenced and determined one's expiration from this dream. We are caught in a delusion about the body's potential transformation, or translation, into various energy forms, which is comparative to shape shifting.

Much of the new age fluffy stuff stimulates a euphoric feeling, it keeps the lethargic program running so that most people seek only to be positive and to look to their guides and masters. It's all part of the game. This is all great for those who are still enjoying this experience; no judgment. The game goes up many levels, however. The kind of biotechnology and "Psychotronic" technology being born in this age presents a realization of the vulnerability of one's mind and one's vessel; the easy manipulation and engineering of the unaware human. This is not new. Humans are now mimicking the mysterious guests of the planet from so long ago. It is why we continue to worship external forces. It is why we debate whether there are neighbors in outer space or not, it is why everything is so unbelievable to us because the general program supports a restricted perception; it's a limiting set of beliefs about what we are and what our capabilities are.

What we must also understand is that such beings were not the peak of magnificence in cosmic technology, they may have been more advanced than those they reengineered on the planet, but it is clear that they were not as highly advanced as we have made them out to be. Although the Annunaki were able to live long life spans, and had a fairly progressive level of technology, it is clear that perhaps their consciousness was not so highly evolved. These kinds of actions would be child's play to more highly advanced beings. To create a universe is a completely transcended level of advancement. As humans, we are challenged by our diluted memory and our non-expansiveness of the mind. We find it challenging to wrap our minds around the fact that there are beings capable of such technology; we call them God! What if you are one of those gods who has ingeniously created a way to experience what you have created without completely being submerged in your creation? Through an illusory act of separatism, or division of self, the process of experiencing this reality became possible and now here you are in your game.

We debate and start wars over whose spiritual belief is right or wrong, yet it is all our creation. We tend to get stuck on every belief that we take in, but much of it limits us. What is your response to this article? Much can be learned about our limitations by examining our response to not only this article, but of concepts that step beyond the limitations of our box. Who are you? That is the question and the response when clarity will not be based on a definition of yourself handed to you by your minister, guru, ascended master, or anyone or anything outside of yourself. What do you feel? What are my limitations in the things that I choose to know? Am I satisfied? You should never be satisfied; we should always be thirsty for more. What's your focus? Are you crying for validation because of the color of your skin or because of racial, spiritual, or political programs? Do you measure your level of spirituality when you speak, or do you evaluate just how spiritual someone is? What are your distractions?

For those whose livelihood dictates whether they can evolve or replace old beliefs, it may be time for them to examine this. There are many in the so termed, spiritual or consciousness movement, whose income depends on remaining with limiting beliefs. Stepping too far outside the box doesn't always sell as well. Pushing and selling fear is a money maker. Creating a fluffy comfy reality is also a money maker. There is an endless list of disempowering concepts that people crave and someone has to provide or support those demands. This should not be interpreted as a judgment of right or wrong, for the game is all encompassing. This is an observation that might speak to someone who is now asking those questions of themselves. There might be great fear in knowing how one's financial transition will occur, should one step away from that, which no longer serves you; know that the fear of being in lack is just that. There is a bridge to cross when we transition to new ground. Stepping upward in awareness will bear greater fruit stimulated by old experiences. The old experiences are the known, and so there is security, however, it served as a stepping stone to higher ground.

We are on a wheel of themes. These cycles present us with themes. This can be seen through astrology as we recognize the theme of each house. The following is a quote from Kelly Roper, Horoscope Group Editor.

> *Ancient astrologers mapped out the heavens into 12 sectors or "houses". When you look at a birth chart, you'll see it's also divided into 12 sectors, one for each house. As the constellations and planets move across the heavens, they pass through individual houses, charging them with their energy. These surges, whether they turn out to have a positive or negative effect, are felt in our daily lives. The influence is strongest when a planet enters its "home base"; the house it rules.*

These themes are frequency driven. From one house to the next, the energies are cycling through the outcome. Being online with this greater *smart grid* can greatly influence the degree to which we expand our consciousness as a species, or as an individual source of power. It is important to understand that these cycles technically do not limit us, but our perception of their influence, along with our commitment to adhering to the control of these cycles, establishes illusionary boundaries. These boundaries then force us to convince ourselves that we cannot cross them, at least not without the navigation of the stars!

Sacred geometry and the platonic solids represent the skeletal structure of the grâter matrix within which the smaller matrix of our universe is housed. These are not the ultimate core structures of existence for there are no structures. Most scientific researchers and discoveries are only investigating this greater matrix although we are inclined to believe that these discoveries are core findings. We have not even scratched the tip of the iceberg!

Is DNA really the port of communication beyond those time related cycles? Is DNA the code translator that opens up greater lines of communication beyond time and space once the signal is given that we are ready to be propelled beyond this level of the game? Is this what is called junk DNA; a network of communication ports?! This maya called reality is held in place by a network of cycles, it is the only way to create the illusion of time. The following is a quote from the book Spiritual Genome written by Brad Bartholomew;

> *Firstly, it has been discovered by a group of Russian scientists, led by Drs. P. Gariaev & V. Poponin, that the DNA has a mysterious resonance. These scientists beamed laser light through a DNA sample, which caused a certain wave pattern to appear on a screen at the rear. However, when the physical DNA sample was removed from the experiment, another wave pattern appeared on the screen at the rear as if there was still a physical sample of DNA present. This same experiment was repeated several times and the same results obtained. They termed this experiment the DNA Phantom Effect. There is some resonating energy in the DNA that is outside of the conventional, four dimensional 'space-time' scenario.*
>
> *The Russian scientists also found that the 95% plus of human DNA that does not code for protein synthesis, so-called 'junk DNA', is*

actually structured like a language, and would therefore be capable of information storage. Indeed it is possible to capture the information patterns in the genes using laser light, and then transfer those information patterns from one genome to another, without the need for the cutting and splicing of chemical genes. By simply transmitting the data via laser light to a different genome they were able to convert a frog embryo into a salamander embryo. The Russian scientists came to the conclusion that the human chromosome acts as a solitonic-holographic computer.

Life is ultimately run by a cosmic computer with high level engineers and programmers on all levels. The human experience is just another running program, a virtual experience. Is there such an objective as beating the game or perhaps overriding the common human program? These are questions we must also ask, but we must also understand that our aim is never about escape but about transcending the lower frequency of the experience. This is a beautifully designed cosmic game and it is important to move into an understanding and appreciation for this magnificent creation. The game wants us to discover all that it can be and where it can take us. Until we can stretch our minds beyond the standard protocols, we will potentially remain on the hamster wheel of these cycles. Stepping outside the safe zone is not for everyone in this lifetime perhaps, but for those who see the bigger picture it can become the momentum to break protocol! You are exactly where you need to be in this moment and if you are reading this article it is indeed not by chance. Always find the code!

9

It Is Our Perception of Time That Binds Us to Our Static View of the Physical

Why speak with such authority about the nature of time followed by contradictions about one's mortality? This is a common way of thinking among many, including our scientists. We live under primitive concepts and beliefs, although we are making evolutionary leaps in technology and in our understanding of consciousness. The concept of time is a core component if we are to penetrate the world of matter by mastership of this science. In each of us, the subject of health plays a significant role in reducing the density of the body in order to align and to travel with the expanding consciousness. However, health must be addressed from perspectives beyond our oral intake of food. What we consume is ultimately not the deciding factor, but rather the density of one's beliefs, perceptions, and the model of reality constructed.

Our engrained perception of time and mortality limits the cycles of these physical bodies. The body expires most often from the density of forms, beliefs, and perceptions interpreted as ill health or disease. There is also ancestral and bloodline density. Aging by deterioration is evidence of our view of time. To age doesn't have to mean decay, but rather a less dense body cycling through the experience of the physical world with the ability to move in and out of this concept of time. This is the magic of ascending in understanding and in memory. Investing energy worrying about meeting timelines for ascension and for 2012 becomes just another matrix for the journey is fluid. We travel and meet our journey according to our own expansiveness. The year 2012 marks the ending of a great cosmic matrix cycle as it relates to this collective space.

There is, indeed, an impact on the consciousness of the planet as a new wave emerges, bringing a new cycle of programs for the evolving planet. These cycles present us with a model of time, for without the concept of time there could be no cycles. There is much that should be observed and questioned here. These cycles are simply a navigation system designed to change the direction of the game, much like a multiple disk player. After each song is played, it moves to the next song until it completes a full cycle. You may hit reset and play the same songs again, or new songs which will also run through a cycle. However, this emerging cycle does present an opportunity for a deeper awareness to emerge among the masses. This high voltage coming through can be used as a conduit. After all, the new song being played is about an evolution in consciousness. Contrary to popular belief, this is something that will occur on various levels for each being.

Must we be regulated by these cycles? This is a question that no one really asks, at least not outwardly. To ask questions that are completely outside the scope of popularity by scientists, as well as the general populace, is to shake your own self out of this deep sleep. Common questions don't do the trick; it's the outrageous questions that zap you beyond the comfort zone of this cosmic game. This cosmic game might not necessarily be quite what we think it is...it almost never is!

10

Spiritual Exhaustion
*Speechless, exhausted, a little ticked off, and thinking what the *%#@*

Is there ever a moment when there is truly nothing left to give? Most everyone has experienced that moment of spiritual exhaustion. It's that feeling of having tried repeatedly, yet things seem to take two steps forward and three steps back. The idea of being positive becomes even more exasperating, especially when others enforce this idea in an attempt to be encouraging. It is the journey through the valley and into the dark night. What is perhaps perplexing is the certainty held in believing that one has exceeded a reoccurrence of that experience. One is left speechless, exhausted, a little ticked off, and thinking *what the *%#@*. It is a very interesting place to be as there is no desire to utilize anything that you know, or have learned, or thought that you understood. This is, indeed, spiritual exhaustion; for you have been trying, and doing, and learning, and falling, and getting up, and dusting yourself off. Perhaps this time you don't quite know how to get back up, or if you even care about getting back up. Ah the journey!

So how do you recover from this tiresome trek? How do you create momentum and reignite passion in moving forward? To examine the synchronicities in one's life along with the disappointments which have created great opportunities in one's life; such as a relocation/move or new friends, a new career or job, love, and a deeper awareness of yourself, perhaps even an exploration of your inner demons. These gifting experiences can be a great reminder and can also shed light on those dimly lit moments. Every disappointment holds purpose. Every set back might actually propel you forward. Our perceptions get the best of us. When things don't unfold as planned or perceived, we are strangled by the uncertainty of the outcome.

Sometimes sharing your feelings with others might actually add fuel to the fire, and you may come away feeling even more frustrated. Most often we are aware of the response that may come from the individual we elect to share our current dilemma. It's best not to open yourself up to what you do not wish to hear, and should you do so knowing the outcome, then what is said to you is exactly what you needed to hear despite your displeasure. Listen closely to what is being said, for there are answers coded in what has been said. The appropriate character with just the right personality steps forward to assist by translating data that is already in you, information that you cannot readily see or access at the moment. Everything, every situation, and everyone, including your environment, is providing you with the data necessary to be decoded for change.

So every certainty and every uncertainty is establishing a pathway that is aligned with our desires and perceptions. How many times have you been disappointed about the timing of things, but it turns out that when things did unfold it was perfect timing? There are also challenges in knowing when to push against the grain and when not to. When there is discomfort in any action and fear, it's best to stop and examine the core of such feelings. If there is satisfaction in doing nothing, then follow that feeling, for your head will encourage you to respond based on fear but your heart will direct you to the patch that is necessary for growth. One might say that you followed your heart in matters of love and you were severely hurt; well that was the experience needed. Deep down there are certain truths which we are aware of in regards to the people that we become involved with, but we take the journey anyway. What we come away with are necessary experiences.

Spiritual exhaustion is generally centered on patterns; relentless patterns in our lives. We continue to come full circle back to the same old experiences again and again. When this happens, one can view it as an opportunity to avoid all previous choices associated with the patterns. Begin breaking the cycle of investing in the same old choices, otherwise patterns get caught in a loop that will continuously return to you. This is a powerful method of recovery. It is evident that all previous choices have created a specific path of outcomes which simply repeat. When this happens, those solutions are short lived and they dead end and bounce back.

This process emphasizes the necessity in breaking limiting habits. A habit is a pattern. Spiritually progressive beings seem to have their lives rattled into intense changes...why is that? When one sets out on a journey of inner discovery, it is challenging to explore great depths when one is encumbered by old programs, beliefs, and perceptions. This clearing then becomes necessary in order to see the path. Not everyone greets this seemingly forced change with ease; some will struggle to hold on to the old. In doing so, we limit the momentum for progression as our eyes and minds become more fixed on what might appear to be a struggle for survival.

What is meant by "spiritual", most especially in this context? It is not the spirit that is exhausted, but rather the struggle to remain in alignment with the spirit. We are emotionally overcome with the frequency or energy of the physical world, no differently than an addiction. We are up against an addiction to the vibration of physicality. The physical world is an addictive experience when in a physical body for any length of time. We are chemically addicted to the experience being processed through the five senses or more. This is a struggle between the visible and the invisible realm, as we belong to both. The visible is, however, a byproduct of the invisible. We are overcome by the density of the physical, and that density is replicated in the body as a result of our thought process, stored and trapped emotions, beliefs, and unresolved matters, as we travel through this virtual game of time and space.

Spiritual exhaustion is then a result of this relentless redemption of a more expansive existence or a more expansive self. How we elect to interpret our experiences makes all the difference in where we go from here. It makes all the difference in determining just how long one will remain in spiritual exhaustion, for if the gift of change being presented is not embraced, the challenges may appear even greater. Reality is a game of perceptions. How does one determine that which begs to be changed? The circumstances being presented is the vehicle of opportunity for change. More specifically, if this is a familiar pattern, then the choices previously used to resolve this matter must be examined, for those choices no longer serve you. Should one elect the same old choices out of fear or desperation, the loop will not break but will move along a path much like a race track until it makes its way back to where it started.

What we fear most is losing control of one's self, or of one's world crumbling. Losing control is a gift, for it is the automated self that has been controlling things all along. It controls based on learned experiences and learned resolutions. It makes choices based on its programming for survival. When that kind of control is lost, and fear is absent, we can more clearly see the truth of the smoke and mirrors that we fight to hold on to. We can hear and feel our more expansive self from which solutions will come. What may seem to be the worst possible outcome could be the best possible outcome for one's opinion; for the best outcome is most often built on the survival program. It all works.

Every situation has something in it for us; there is always a gift to be retrieved. All of life is synchronistic; each moment aligns with the next to meet the conditions of your journey. What are the conditions of your journey? Is it to continue the same experiences until you expire? Is it to fight against change? Is it to be limited in your perceptions and beliefs? Is it to go the unlimited extra mile? If it is indeed to go the unlimited extra mile, then stepping outside of the box is a prerequisite to freeing our minds and bodies. The illusionary boundaries of time will be made clear, for all of our actions and addictions are tied into our perception or programming of time. It is why we coddle the physical in fear of running out of time. It is why the survival program works so well, for we fear nonexistence; this is a core program in all human beings. This program can also be a gift in propelling us to discover more about whom we are and our potential to exceed time as we have embraced it.

Spiritual exhaustion can be a great gift at this moment, for it is a grand opportunity to release, change, and become less dense. It is an opportunity for tremendous vibrational shifts. While experiencing this process will simply allow one's self to feel, express, and allow emotions to play out, don't fight them with positive thinking. Let them emerge so that you can see exactly what is at the root of your belief system; it's an opportunity to see the inner saboteurs of one's life. These are the emotions we fight against in attempting to remain positive, as we do battle with doubt. Positivity must come freely unencumbered by doubt. Doubt is also a gift. Unveiling the master within is the gift of the journey and only you can bring forth what you already are. It's the great work and so when we ask the question of how we can change the world, we must take it to heart that the world is only being experienced by each of us according to the conditions of our journey. It always comes back to the individual. Ultimately, spiritual exhaustion is about the unveiling of the master within; it is the key to experiencing the world on new levels of perception. Find the gift!

11

Honoring Who You Are

To own who you are in every moment and to honor your truth without fear of ridicule is an extremely freeing experience. This can be accomplished without imposing our truth on others, unless invited to share. Honoring one's truth is also about realizing that it is not necessary to debate or to defend your position. Debating, defending, and sharing are very different experiences. If there is fear in owning one's truth we should then seek to understand what it is that is feared or speculated about the potential outcome. To be who you are is not about bravery, it is simply about being who you are; you are a reflection of your understanding.

Operating from a perspective of needing to save the world, and taking it on as your personal mission, is really about your need to experience what it would be like to be a superhero. The stage is always set and the characters are always there to support all experiences. Saving the world/people is a common sentiment most often experienced at some point in our awakening. Most often, this is a result of the excitement felt as we grow into a more profound memory of who we are. Awakening from that space of thinking can propel us back to our inner connection as we shift away from the energy expelled externalizing. To observe the game while participating in it can establish opportunities, although viewed as challenges, they can become opportunities. We then no longer live from a mindset of endless challenges but rather from the perspective of opportunities and growth. How do you test the boundaries or the freedom of what is known unless there are simulations? To honor one's truth is to test the very brim of time and space (despite its nonexistence).

So, remember that classifying your actions as bravery has nothing to do with simply honoring who you are. Throughout history, great leaders have stepped into positions despite the apparent danger, but they were simply being who they were. If your perception is about doing battle, or being an advocate, understand the energy in which you stand, as this is a warring planet. Everything in this context of reality is about opposition and opponents. However, to stand in representation of your awareness can move mountains without engaging in battles. Battles are about the opposing forces of right and wrong as defined by the human program. Operating from a space of resonance shifts one from a space of judgment, for ultimately, everyone is only responding according to what resonates. We are responding according to the vibration of one's consciousness; the vibration of one's awareness or alertness. Just be!

12

Walking through the valley of Archetypical Reality

The distractions are relentless, simply one after another; the game is hypnotic and engaging. Since the beginning of the 2011 cycle, our minds have been busied with an assortment of distractions. Tsunamis, pirate kidnappings, the royal wedding, Osama bin laden, Lindsay Lohan, Libya, radiation poison, Charlie Sheen, cancer, death, illness, and more. There is not much space in-between to process thoughts which plunge below the surface of reality. This is much like going on a guided tour, and the guide's job is to keep the excitement moving as he wants to be sure that he delivers your money's worth. After a while, the traveler is tired from the day's events, as there is much to process; yet there are a great many unregistered occurrences not part of our conscious experience. In each moment, our minds are bombarded by projections. The question should then be asked: What is it that wasn't seen as the events of the day moved along in this successive sequence? This is the manner in which most experience life on a daily basis, enclosed in a bubble of distractions.

What is not realized is that we are a well-ordered package of ideas (data) which steadily continues to be implemented by leaders and rulers of civilizations and societies. We struggle to hold on to this conceptual reality program. We struggle to hold on to the blue print, and to hold on to the social, religious, and corporate imprints. Our lives are archetypical, and because of this we live within the boundaries of predictabilities. We are the result of all preceding civilizations, molded and shaped by design into a model which represents today's human. Redefining the meaning of evolution plays an important role as we seek to broaden our understanding. Are we evolved because we use a knife, fork, and plate? Are we evolved because we don't hunt and kill our own food? Are we evolved because we have a spiritual or religious belief or program? Are we evolved because we channel other beings? Are we evolved because we eat raw food? Are we evolved because we wear clothes? Are we evolved because we use credit cards or have money? Are we evolved because those that rule tell us so? What is evolution? Evolution is defined as a process of development. Perhaps it is more a sense of primal sophistication when we truly examine the advancements held by previous cultures which exceeded our own. We are a society obsessed with topical value. This acts as a covering over our fears about discovering the technology of our design. There is bias in our ability to examine the spectrum of possibilities in how we came to be (in human form that is).

FROM THE MATRIX:

> **Trinity:** I know why you're here, Neo. I know what you've been doing...why you hardly sleep, why you live alone, and why night after night you sit by your computer. You're looking for him. I know because I was once looking for the same thing. And when he found me, he told me I wasn't really looking for him. I was looking for an answer. It's the question that drives us, Neo. It's the question that brought you here. You know the question, just as I did.
> **Neo:** What is the Matrix?
> **Trinity**: The answer is out there, Neo, and it's looking for you, and it will find you if you want it to.

In Greek mythology Morpheus is known as the god of dreams. Neo, prior to his awakening, was operating under the spell of sleep, as most are. His search for Morpheus was symbolic of his realization that his world was not quite what he had been led to believe. So it is with most of us; there is a feeling that the life we see and experience is somehow overshadowing a more profound possibility of one's existence.

So, are we asking questions? Not just one question but many questions. It is the questions which reach in and pulls us out from the belly of archetypical reality. Our path of questioning is further infiltrated by a programmed arrangement of reality woven into the mind. To ask questions that exceed the preset collective programs becomes the code to unlocking that part of us that seems to have been held hostage or imprisoned.

In this polarized reality we are sold fear and fluff. We are controlled through both the filter of government, corporations, religions, education, and spiritual fluff, and by those outside of the human game. We are told that "You are in danger but don't worry we have just what you need." People remain confused about what they should hold as a belief while running around outside of themselves; if there is such a thing as *outside*. They become caught in the holographic projection of what appears to be *out there*. Kaiser Permanente has a quote that says *Life is Out there, Get up, Get out and thrive*; this phrase can be decoded by the brain in several different ways. We are reminded that life is not happening inside of us, but outside of ourselves. To experience the fullness of the matrix requires that we buy into the notion of everything being outside of us.

Operating in the mindset of externalizing is the archetypical approach and a necessary response in fully engaging in the matrix of reality. We are playing in a holodeck. The entire structure which we identify as our universe and solar system is an ever changing holodeck, despite our inability to see its interchangeability. This is what scientists are discovering. What they now understand is that reality is holographic.

Where did the word holodeck come from: (taken from Wikipedia) *A holodeck is a simulated reality facility located on starships and starbases in the fictional Star Trek universe. An episode of Star Trek: The Animated Series, "The Practical Joker", formed the groundwork for the idea in the 1970s by portraying a recreation room capable of holographic simulations. The holodeck was first seen in the pilot episode of Star Trek: The Next Generation, "Encounter at Farpoint". The concept of a holodeck was* first shown to humans through an encounter with the Xyrillan race in the Star Trek: Enterprise episode "Unexpected".

The holodeck is depicted as an enclosed room in which objects and people are simulated by a combination of replicated matter, tractor beams, and shaped force fields onto which holographic images are projected.

To say that this is simply a television show for entertainment is to also observe one's limitations. All such concepts explored by the human mind are the result of tapping into the engineering of reality. In a quote from Ray Bradbury science fiction writer; *We are the miracle of force and matter making itself over into imagination and will. Incredible. The Life Force experimenting with forms. You for one. Me for another. The Universe has shouted itself alive. We are one of the shouts.*

What is the magic word, or the realization, that will allow us to experience this interchangeability? It is our ability to question! What questions are you asking? Questions are composed based on the depth of our curious mind. What are you curious about? Are you curious about your existence or of this overall experience we call reality? The extent of what we experience will always be limited to the range of our curiosity and questioning. *"Only those who will risk going too far can possibly find out how far one can go."* — T.S. Eliot

Although one might defend being open and explorative, it would serve to examine the boundaries which may exist regarding the extent to which one may choose to investigate. What are your fears about going deeper? When one draws a final analysis about the nature of reality, such conclusions reflect limitations. When we become conclusive about the nature of the spirit, or of the mind, or of creation, these are clues into our perception base. Our limitations are showing themselves to us, and when realized, this should be viewed as an opportunity to go deeper. In all that is being discovered by, not only scientists, but by all those of a deeper curious nature, it is simply allowing us to experience yet another angle of the many faces of creation. We may perhaps begin to realize that there is never a final analysis.

In walking through the valley of archetypical reality, we must remain aware that when completely submerged, we are limited only to viewing our lives through the filter of the collective model. The word archetypical expresses the *typical architecture* or design of the collective model of reality. To begin to question this construct is to continuously alter this collective model of reality. Without the penetration of questions into the fabric of structured beliefs, we have bound ourselves to the rules in place. We will continue to recreate reality from old memories steaming through the collective data stream, as well as our own unique data bank. In the film *Inception*, a significant quote was "Never recreate from your memory. Always imagine new places!"

Our analysis of each other is also filtered through collective programs. In order to make comparative distinctions of good or bad, right or wrong, rich or poor, there has to be a barometer by which to measure and interpret feelings and emotions. The general holodeck of collective reality is programmed to function based on particular principles. We then respond to those principles through our emotions, drawing conclusions about one another in our prefab environment. To be other than typical, or to operate outside the realm of acceptability, is unnerving for most and we must be clear in understanding what this means. To operate outside the realm of acceptability's does not mean that one cannot work within the corporate environment, or participate in some of the mechanics of this reality. It is about the inner transition and not so much about a topical approach, which simply carry the appearance of freedom. The workplace can be used as an amazing fitness center for ones evolution for one is given an opportunity several times per day to step up their game. This is equivalent to our transformation in the madness of the matrix. We are making our way through, despite the survival program. To recognize each moment and each experience as an opportunity instead of an obstacle can become the magic wand. Leaping into this mindset can be a challenging feat, especially in the beginning of experimenting with this concept. It is, however, a major key in working with the holodeck. It will allow us to experience the interchangeability of reality which is possible on all levels. What we must remember is that it is all about the questions; questions lead to answers which can potentially lead us beyond the valley of typical reality. It is the driving force that is taking us on a journey to see just how deep the rabbit hole goes.

13

The Money Game in the Matrix
The Real Casino

The money game continues to be the tool of measurement by which many determine their own value and worth, as well as those of others. There are master players who are few and far between, while the majority of the world struggles to figure out how to stay in the game, if only as a pawn. Although master players, such as those who reign at the helm of power through governing systems on the planet may appear on the opposite end of lack, it does not mean that they have bypassed the illusion of the monetary matrix. They are simply playing from another level of the monetary game. Have you ever visited Las Vegas, or Atlantic City, or any casino for that matter? What is not realized is that we have been playing the game of life in the biggest casino of them all. This currency aspect of reality is a stratum of the matrix in which everyone conforms to the illusion of money. We are told that money makes the world go round. This is true when interpreted as the force of energy, power or current. Money is ultimately an extension of our own thought projections and life force. It is our thoughts and our life force that is converted into this form of *current* (currency) whether viewed from the perspective of physical labor, or from a projection of the mind, or through strategic planning. Either way this *current* (your life force) streams from you!

How is reality a vast casino? Or one might say a cosmic casino. The world of commerce looks you in the eye and reminds you that without the required monetary increments you won't be able to maintain the essentials for human survival which are food, clothes, and shelter. One's selection of food, clothes, and shelter is, however, sliced into a number of possibilities, each one determined by a specific monetary class. In the game, one's quality of life is subject to your ability to strategize in life's casino, or at least so we are lead to believe.

In order to begin to be more strategic in your game, perhaps it is necessary to examine the casino and gambling elements of the game. Everything that we create outside of us, such as the casinos for gambling, is always a replication of a more obscure aspect of reality. Reality unfolds in levels of subtlety, causing the obvious to be overridden by our aim to meet the demands of the game. We are diehard, addicted game players who do not realize that we embark on a daily gamble. The casino of the matrix has an assortment of games no different than the physical casinos. One chooses the kind of game, or games, you will play and how much you are willing to gamble.

We spend our lives "hoping", just as we do when we sit in front of a slot machine, or at the blackjack table, or watching for the winning numbers of the lottery ticket. As we pull the lever, or roll the dice, or select our lottery numbers, we *hope* for the jackpot or for some level of winning that will solve certain deficiencies in our overall game. So it is with each of us in life's casino. When we awake in the morning we awake ready to dive into the game despite any proclaimed resistance to it. We awaken into the casino *hoping* that today will be a good day at the slot machine or the craps table. We hope that we are not thrown any curve balls for the day. It's all a gamble; not being sure exactly how the day will pan out. Exactly how do we automatically journey into the casino upon waking in the mornings? In the mornings, as we begin returning from the world of sleep, most often you will find yourself already thinking and strategizing about the day's events. The events of the day are your assortment of games that you will play. Each situation, each dilemma, each person, coworkers that you may not be happy with, a job that you hate going into or perhaps you may like going into, a lunch date scheduled for the day, does he or she like you, will you get the loan, relationships, bills to be paid, the party you are planning and the list goes on and on.

Each one of these interactions will shape its own unique game. Throughout the day you may have five or more unique games.

Sometimes the emotions injected into the first game for the day will spill over into all other games. At the end of the day you will have collected an assortment of emotional currency from each one of these experiences, and this is what you take home with you. These are the payoffs from "today's" game. At bedtime you lay in bed and you go over your payoffs for the day and you begin to strategize about your approach in the casino tomorrow, and you do it all over again each day. We believe that we are out working hard at making money but it's not about the money, it has always been about the payoffs. Money doesn't exist in the first place, what does exist are the experiences we associate with sustaining our money supply. Money is a current that responds according to the required payoff of the player.

There are other factors at play which aid in sustaining the actual money program and our belief systems about money. We can examine the commercial system which regulates the operations of our world along with those who designed it. This is the wheel which ensures the illusionary, daily grind as we *hustle* our way to fulfill the requirements of the monetary matrix. The word *hustle* in this context refers to the strategies we incorporate in our game in order to fulfill the illusion of *making* money. Our general definition of street hustling is equal to the hustle established from the boardroom on down. We are all hustling! We are hustling for the payoff despite the stores we attach to our reasons. This is the thrill of life's casino. Each time you roll the dice on a daily basis you *hope* and we become addicted to the rush that is felt from *hoping*, as you step up to play.

We have convinced ourselves that this is the only game in town, and if we do not play it then we are doomed! What will we do! As a reminder, we do not *make* money; for money represents a *currency* stream *"Energy can neither be created nor destroyed, but it can be transformed from one form to the other."* There is NO money being made! The system already knows this but it is the rest of the programmed minds that are completely oblivious to this. We all have walked this road; we have all been taken for a ride. What is important to recognize is that although we are speaking of money, what lies at the core of this experience is how it all relates to our existence. It is said that time is money and there is indeed truth to this. It's all science. Neither time nor money really exists!

Finding a way over this monetary illusion is not about fighting the system. One must go beyond the system through an elevation in consciousness in order to transcend these programs and perception boundaries. Our very language, emotions, and reference points to *money* must change. To understand that we measure our life force in the same manner that we measure money is a powerful realization. We are mechanized in our conclusions of money being scarce or plenty. This is based on a systemic programming of our perception in reference to the world of commerce. We view money as something that runs out, and rightly so. We are continuously reminded of the economy and all things of commercial value as measured based on someone else's conditions. It is only natural that we would be in fear of depletion, as this has been a long standing program. The brain is trained to maintain focus on the monetary codes of scarcity and plenty when measuring currency value. This is an amazing game within which we have gotten lost, as it all seems so believable which it is when submerged in it. It's not about what *they* did, although it helps to understand the strategies that continue to hold our minds spellbound to the concepts of money, worth, and value. J.P. Morgan said "If you have to ask how much it costs, you can't afford it." Author Lex Lobe reminds us that "Morgan knew that he had the ability to create money when needed. Money goes from something that does not exist to something that does." We are the currency that flows through all facets of life.

What the economy is, or is not, are only thought projections which impact the individual according to what their current story calls for. There are a great many that are not impacted by the so called economy. We are dealing with digital projections. This is a psychological game imposed by those who are privy to the money projector. Therefore our minds become entangled in a measurement assessment of cost. Cost is obviously associated with the value we place on the purchase or exchange being pondered. Where does our value system come from? Are you operating based on what truly resonates with you or is it based on the value table provided for us based on coded brands? When we operate based on resonance, scientifically the current should always be there to meet the desire. We can also examine what our desire maybe associated with. This will also make a difference in how the currency unfolds to support the desire. There is an article that came out today February 11, 2011 titled (1) *IMF calls for dollar alternative* by Ben Rooney appearing on CNNMoney.com, this kind of information reminds us of the ability of the coordinators or money magicians to determine what money will be or not be. This becomes another program upload or program adjustment to your pre-existing money program. This kind of upload takes very well, and the people are none the wiser that there is no money, only a suggested belief or perception.

The abundance hype and law of attraction concepts had what we would refer to as "good" intensions. However, there were always so many key ingredients missing that some either became more confused than when they started, or they went to the other extreme of drowning in the hype. It all seemed to become just another cult-like episode. There are also those in the "spiritual" community who have convinced themselves that staying in lack, and asking for donations, is a more "spiritual" approach. Here the table of measurement pops up to evaluate or place you on the spiritual scale. Just how spiritual are you, well let's just measure that. This is based on the same principles of the concept of money that is programmed into to us. We are using the same method of currency measurement to measure spirituality. Everything is spiritual! Many of these people, however, feel guilt in expressing monetary value for their work or services clearly based on their money and spirituality programs. There is no right or wrong, or good or bad, in the perception we choose. This journey is such an amazing experience as one is allowed to take on any character he or she wants to experience. Money is not the evil thing here but rather acts as a catalyst. It supports each of our perceptions. Our deep rooted perceptions about money are only a reflection of the foundation upon which our individual games are being played. It is the shape of our core story from which we live our lives. Money is a phantom and represents the current which flows from us. We are dealing with quantum states. An analogy can be drawn from the EPR Experiment of (2) *Schrödinger's Cat*. It can certainly be applied to our observation and conclusions of what is or isn't. The power of suggestion influences the mind of the observer establishing predetermined notions of that which is to be observed; in this case money.

We can perhaps begin to take an honest look at our stories, our perceptions, and the current methods of playing the game. Changing the game is therefore possible, despite our addiction to the payoffs; and when the payoffs no longer serve us, only then will we embark on change in creating a new reality.

14

2012 - A Dismantling of Old Codes and Programs

There is much discussion about 2012, and as the time draws closer, discussions are increasing globally and now spilling over into the main stream population. There is, however, a common understanding among most all religions. They all conclude that there is an end coming.

Is it an end to the planet itself? No. It is, however, an end to the old design concept of human experiences. When planets such as earth are created, they are designed based on specific concepts or themes. They are systems with architectural designs based on a blueprint of intended experiences for life forms born to the system. These systems operate within a certain range of frequency or vibration. The planet's Electromagnetic Field (EMF) determines the colors, tones, and light frequencies for our planet. In other words, life in those systems will only be exposed to certain frequency patterns of color, light, and sound. Our brains will only connect with specific frequencies of color, light, and sound patterns unless an individual transcends these perimeters.

We have carried out the human experience possibly from all potentials. The Mayan calendar shows the countdown to the end of this fourth cycle. We are in the fourth cycle of the greater 104,000 year cycle; four smaller cycles of 26,000 years. There is an overall greater growth expansion in our solar system and the overall Universe. These are natural timers in place like an hour glass. The larger system of which we are apart requires a new level of data from systems operating in this level of vibration. When this occurs, a graduation process takes place as new concepts and systems will be birthed. The planet is currently in a readjustment process, receiving the essential stream of information from the Sun which stands as the translator of specific codes or patterns fed to the planet from a more central sun;

the main power plant for our system. There has been an increase in solar flares which are very much related to the much dreaded global warming. It is important that we no longer view this occurrence from a fantasy standpoint, but rather from the depth of who you are as a cosmic traveler; astronaut/scientist/spirit/source. Recognize that all things are simply energy patterns based on specific codes/packets of energy, or formulas supportive of the intended form. Although scientists remain baffled they continue to slowly make ground breaking discoveries. However when we the none scientist begin to see more deeply we will find ourselves a step ahead of these scientific discoveries

"IMAGE data, translated into visuals by computer, shows the superheated gas called plasma streaming from the Sun and hitting the Earth's outer atmosphere. Most is deflected but some starts a reaction with the atmosphere itself. It shows bursts of hydrogen and oxygen coming out of Earth's atmosphere." Stephen Fuselier, manager of the Space Physics Laboratory at Lockheed-Martin Advanced Technology Center in Palo Alto, California, told reporters. "The timing is most important - there is a direct input from the solar wind. The Earth responds immediately by ejecting a part of the atmosphere. It is a very small part," Fuselier stresses "a stream of charged oxygen atoms. Each storm accounts for about 100 tons of oxygen expelled into space. That is about the air volume in the Louisiana Superdome," he said. "That sounds like a lot by human standards but in fact Earth's atmosphere is much, much larger than that." He said even billions of years of storms would not measurably deplete the atmosphere.

The moment it hits space, this oxygen becomes super-charged in bursts that can also be "seen" by IMAGE. Some of it loops backs into the atmosphere, but much gets caught up in the solar wind and is carried away. "It has gained 100,000 times the energy it had when it left the atmosphere, so it is very pumped up." Fuselier said. "When it plunges into the atmosphere, these strong currents are generated. They transform the mid-latitudes from their usual calm state into kind of a maelstrom that has direct effects on our daily lives." Such storms have knocked entire power grids offline and can interrupt radio broadcasts and satellite signals - including global positioning satellite or GPS technology relied upon by hikers, marine traffic, and soldiers in the field.

"This is how space storms reach down into the Earth and touch our daily lives," John Foster of the Massachusetts Institute of Technology Haystack Observatory said.

In my book, The Holographic Canvas, there is a chapter titled "Oxygen and the Transformation of Reality", from the article above, the transmitting and receiving process through breath is evident. What is it that is most evident in a diseased body? The lack of oxygen. Disease/parasites/ etc. can only exist in a minimally oxygenated body. Cells die from the lack of oxygen; the brain will not function properly when minimally oxygenated. Currently, we are scurrying to make changes to our environment due to the diminished quality of air and life. Despite this global fear, is it possible to supersede this visible environmental decline in 3D? Yes! Let go of the fantasy! Many, many distractions related to the old concept will increasingly present themselves as there are a number of potential endings that have been written into the 2012 closure. Life is both an experiment and an experience, and although the old game/concept will come to an end for some, it does not mean that it will come to an end in the minds of many. Quite a few will hold the old format, or blueprint, in their being as we have all grown comfortable with these old programs. Such beings will continue to live a variation of the old concepts associated with the old. This will be comparable to a recorded past, an old hologram, one that will be played over and over again until it is realized that they have been living in the past. Well guess what...this is what we have been living. This is the past! For some, there is a sense of living in the past. This life is but a memory an old memory! These cycles come and go, creating cyclic portals for those wishing to exit the past and move forward into a freer and more fluid experience. As the brain shifts out of the mode of rewind, new neuro pathways are created in the brain. Magnetic fields have been proven to promote the growth of neurons in certain areas of the brain. Here is a quote taken from The Holographic Canvas:

"The brain operates off of electrical signals in the form of an image. Sensory stimuli are processed in the brain as a stream of electrical impulses created by neurons firing. Neurons are a group of cells specializing in specific functions such as the assembly of blood, organs, glands, bones etc. The body is comprised of billions of cells, which categorically form the entire organism; however, the brain includes billions of neurons, which begin "firing" messages upon stimuli of the five senses. These messages are in the form of hormones, chemicals, and electrical impulses."

Here is another quote taken from Electrical Design in the Human Body by Craig Savige:

"The basic building block of the nervous system is the nerve cell, called a neuron. The brain itself consists primarily of neurons. Under a microscope a neuron looks like an octopus with many tentacles. A neuron can transmit an electrical impulse to the next neuron. The network of electrical impulses enables us to receive information from the physical world and then send it to our brains, and vice versa. Without the neuron circuits, our bodies would completely shut down, like turning off the power supply to a city."

The harnessing of oxygen in our bodies supported by deep awareness will allow the transformation of the chemicals/hormones in the body to expand in alignment with the current transformation of

Earth. You will never feel the extreme changes in Earth's temperatures, as your body will operate in alignment. It is also important to remember that fifty million years ago the entire planet held global tropical temperatures. We did not have four seasons. The tilt in the Earth's axis allowed another aspect of the experience to be had. Human emotions are completely affected by atmospheric changes. The slightest tilt or solar changes will impact on these streams of electrical impulses from which emotions are constructed.

Another seldom unaddressed aspect of human biology is that there is magnetite in the human brain. A Caltech geobiologist, Joseph Kirschivink, discovered magnetic crystals in human brain tissue now called magnetite. Through the use of a high resolution transmission microscope they discovered that there were at least five million magnetite crystals in a thimble full of brain tissue, each of which were approximately a millionth of an inch long. They further discovered that when this magnetite was exposed to strong electric fields they could readjust themselves, and either open or force these channels shut. The following quote may assist in supporting my conclusion of the manner in which the Sun acts as a convertor of energy and a transmitter as well, which would also be evidence of the impact of the electrical currents from the Sun upon the Earth's magnetic field, as well as upon the magnetite in our brains. (Taken from the Electric Sky, discoveries by Ralph Juergens):

"The Sun may be powered, not from within itself, but from outside, by the electric (Birkeland) currents that flow in our arm of our galaxy as they do in all galaxies. This possibility that the Sun may be externally powered by its galactic environment is the most speculative idea in the ES hypothesis and is always attacked by critics while they ignore all the other explanatory properties of the ES model. In the Plasma Universe model, these cosmic sized, low-density currents create the galaxies and the stars within those galaxies by the electromagnetic z-pinch effect. It is only a small extrapolation to ask whether these currents remain to power those stars. Galactic currents are of low current *density*, but, because the sizes of the stars are large, the total current (Amperage) is high. The Sun's radiated power at any instant is due to the energy imparted by that amperage. As the Sun moves around the galactic center it may come into regions of higher or lower current density and so its output may vary both periodically and randomly."

I understand that the information being presented is not written in a manner filled with mysticism and fantasy the way that many are accustomed to having their spiritual uplift. I am led to write this information in a manner that is shifting away from the old process as part of the shifting into a more fluid consciousness with each and every traveler owning his/her journey and your responsibility to your own awakening. Through this non-mystical process, the brain begins to dismantle the current holographic illusion. The brain remains in constant contact with all fields of existence, and with this shifting away from the old hologram, the brain is signaled to begin to allow the individual to enter new fields of thought and consciousness and worlds. The limitation under which we have been experiencing 3D life, based on a predesigned system, will now become clear to some allowing one to fluidly experience a more expansive life. For too long we have buried ourselves in the rendering of our lives, and spiritual growth to forces outside of ourselves. There is no one responsible for your evolution but you. You came on this journey of your own free will and you must ascend into your memory of who you are as a sovereign being. You created a concept of what Earth would be and then you entered your own design, your own game, became your own children now lost in the experience. You are the ascended masters you seek. Our blinders and spiritual amnesia, however, have made it challenging for us to see or to remember. This cyclic transition presents us with an opportunity to leap into the future which, to some degree, is our distant past.

That transitional moment is upon us right now. Do not wait for 2012 based on any calendar because time is of a magical nature and we are in the midst of this great change. Just remember that there are many distractions coming your way, many of which will be extreme potions of fear and snake oil money cures. Money will be one of the biggest catalysts, the biggest ma-trix of illusion. The new age, metaphysical movement, will be the vehicle through which much of this ma-trix will play out. Such numerical concepts as 11:11 are codes pre-wired into the brain. Such codes serve the purpose of monitoring, uploading, and downloading.

Symbols are the most significant language to the human brain as much more can be conveyed to the brain than a million words ever could. The codes11:11, 11:22, etc. became more prevalent to the new age community over the past fifteen to twenty years as part of the cyclic transition in place. We must keep in mind that the human brain is no less programmable than any computer. Many things are downloaded into human consciousness more easily according to the frequency of brain wave patterns, or even chemically induced shifts in the brain can alter one's will. Many have had the 11:11 experience and for some it occurs several times per day. Human consciousness has always been monitored, and it increases as we move towards this transition. This evaluation of consciousness is to determine the growth process, have we progressed enough to be a threat to those requiring the continuation of the old Earth experiment. This evaluation is of course an upload process. Certain vibration of information is then downloaded if one is in an open and embracing state for these codes. Many are. Most often when we interact with 11:11, it is while we are driving, sitting, or are in some sort of focused yet relaxed mode. We are generally never jumping around. Brain waves need to be in a certain alterable frequency. When there is a group held focus on 11:11, these willing minds bring in downloads that present another illusion of freedom that impacts the collective field as more fantasy is conjured up. We are manipulated like small children/infants excited to receive goodies from our older siblings.

Numbers are undoubtedly the formula through which all things exist. For all things are based on a measurement of energy forming frequency patterns. What many fail to realize is the programmed system or hologram within which the experience has been played out as we readily surrender to the latest spiritual hype. This has been a system that has operated based on layers of programs and concepts with further programming orchestrated by other human beings in positions of control over vulnerable minds. This may all sound farfetched, but should you decide to peel the onion of your life, and what you have believed based on collective beliefs, it will all become clear. If you can center yourself without the impact of your emotions or your ego, you will see an old system that is on its way out so that you can be free to allow yourself to be worthy of being an unlimited being. Open your mind, ignite your spirit, choose wisely for choices that are made harnessing the old concept will not be realized for quite some time, as no one will be the wiser that they have not shifted. Listen to your own inner guidance, not guides or gurus, but your own God/Source within you that you ultimately are.

The year 2012 is simply the ending of the old themes by which this reality was designed. There is a new Earth, a different time, a different concept. A number of you have probably faced some difficulties and confusion in shifting away from these "light worker" roles which you have used as your identity for quite some time. Losing our identity is difficult, as we no longer know what to say when someone says, "What do you do?" You can now free yourself to be something different, not a "light worker", not a metaphysician, not a healer or a channel, not any one thing! You can free yourself to shift into new experiences. The transition can, at times, be difficult both financially and emotionally, most often forcing us to return to the old; but going backwards can also cause greater pain. You may also experience frustration, confusion and emotional challenges as the old is no longer working for you. Much of those feelings are based on the old Earth design, social programs, family programs, religious programs that are now short circuiting in opposition to being replaced with the new. This is happening in order to present one with the opportunity to embark on the new. Your brain's slate is being wiped clean to be re-wired with the new should you allow the process to take place. This transition is not for the faint of heart, so do not be hard on yourself if you find that it is just too much. Dismantling programs thousands of years old can be torturous although one need only let go and allow, or not allow.

Remember that it's only a game, one that appears to have lasted for eons, but in the magic motion of time, it has only been but a moment.

15

Playing It Safe

I wrote an article, not realizing the stir it would have generated. The article was titled <u>Enough with this "Blissed" out Agenda</u>. There were many who felt inspired by it and there were a few who came at me as if I was the Antichrist. Those who were inspired were those who apparently had drawn the same conclusions, as I had never really voiced it, at least not in an open forum. I, however, voiced it, yet this was not the first time. No, I did not play it safe. I recognize that many are hungry for something else, but when all that seems to be there is the same old same old, then some will hang in there in silence, and some will retreat quietly to themselves. One focus point of the article addressed the art of channeling and its followers. Those who were annoyed with the article seemed to be those who were avid supporters of channeling, or those who simply just did not agree for whatever their reasons were.

Before going further with this article, let me say very clearly once again that all of it is valid, this cannot be stressed enough. We are operating according to what we find essential and appropriate. This also does not mean that one is superior over the other, or that one is lesser or greater, or that one is chosen and the other not. The writing of that article was all by design, and everyone who read it did so for a reason regardless of the opinion which was formed. There are no mistakes! It is advisable that one ask themselves why they were prompted to read it…and I must ask myself why I wrote it and why did I choose to put myself out there in this manner. Well I have certainly had to grow a thick layer of skin since then. Was I upset when I wrote the article? No. It is the reason for the humorous style in approaching the subject matter.

I have learned that to play it safe when it comes to my own evolution and what I am feeling inside is to deny myself the opportunity to grow by leaps and bounds…to avoid misinterpretation; let me clarify that this statement applies to me; I cannot speak for anyone else. However, I realize the manner in which playing it safe can limit one to a predictable set of possibilities. Predictability is a safe space, it is the familiar. It is why many find it challenging to let go of the past despite the challenges of the past, nonetheless, the past provides a reference point for predictable outcomes. This creates the rewind effect. Every next moment is then created from the patterns of the past with slight variations to the experience. Others will say but "sometimes you need to play it safe" that could be defined perhaps as diplomacy. Yes I agree, so it is then up to the individual to determine when to apply the brakes and when to hit the gas.

We are all very protective of our holograms, by that I mean our individual construct of reality. It is the reason why we are ready to defend it. Our holograms are guarded by our egos. We come out with heavy artillery as we are our own military for our reality; we must fight to protect it at all cost from all foreign invaders. We stand guard ready to zone in on that one word or that one look that signals opposition, this of course activates the defense system. We are programmed to survive; our survival program is running 24/7, it is why most of our society operates on a daily basis in the survival mode, the "fight or flight" mode. This entire process is duplicated in the overall hologram; countries fighting to defend themselves from foreign invaders. Again, much misunderstanding has set off many wars. It's always about a fight to defend our county, our land, our territory, our religious/spiritual beliefs, our culture, and of course our planet from foreign invaders. This is what we all do. Again this, is not a judgment, this is an observation. Defend it if you will for in that moment you will see the very thing that I am speaking of. In truth and in fact what are we defending? Do we really know what it is that we are defending? Yet all of it is the nature of the experience on the planet. The entire spectrum of experiences navigates us through our goal in exploring the full range of possibilities in being human. So in other words, being in survival mode or not being in survival mode is ok either way. We are experiencing the range according to what is needed. I too found myself wanting to defend myself, defend the article, but from what? Would I be defending myself from not playing it safe? The experience was what I created for myself. There was no hiding; it was a matter of owning my expression. It gave me new dimension into myself and where I go from here.

It is the physical part of us that does the reacting. These bodies are the vehicle designed for the processing of these experiences, it processes a chemical response; electrochemical impulses. These bodies are designed to "survive", to protect itself from invaders. We have, however, turned over complete control to these bodies, and so much of our thoughts and actions are run by the "survival" system in place. We are on autopilot. It is why our diets can destroy the body, it is because the frequency of the thought field and belief systems are of an equivalent vibration and therefore unable to override or penetrate the frequency patterns of the substance being ingested. We have stabilized foods to particular frequencies as can be observed in its form and its chemical makeup. We are unable to un-stabilize the molecular patterns to the realization that "there is no spoon, it is you that bends". This is what we are all working towards regardless of the road we may take, regardless of what we are aware of. It is about coming to the realization that there is no spoon. This analogy is supported by breakthroughs in quantum physics. It is the observer that creates the illusion of the bending spoon.

Here is a quote from The Holographic Universe by Michael Talbot:

> "University of London physicist David Bohm, for example, believes Aspect's findings imply that objective reality does not exist, that despite its apparent solidity the Universe is at heart a phantasm, a gigantic and splendidly detailed

hologram. To understand why Bohm makes this startling assertion, one must first understand a little about holograms.

A hologram is a three-dimensional photograph made with the aid of a laser. To make a hologram, the object to be photographed is first bathed in the light of a laser beam. Then a second laser beam is bounced off the reflected light of the first and the resulting interference pattern (the area where the two laser beams co-mingle) is captured on film. When the film is developed, it looks like a meaningless swirl of light and dark lines. But as soon as the developed film is illuminated by another laser beam, a three-dimensional image of the original object appears.

The three-dimensionality of such images is not the only remarkable characteristic of holograms. If a hologram of a rose is cut in half and then illuminated by a laser, each half will still be found to contain the entire image of a rose. Indeed if the halves are divided again, each snippet of film will always be found to contain a smaller but intact version of the original image. Unlike normal photographs, every part of a hologram contains all the information possessed by the whole."

It is clear to me that a number of people will agree to this realization, yet in the same breath this will be contradicted. This recognition of this phantom/holographic design of reality clearly imposes the realization that creation is like a child playing hide and go seek with itself. Growing up basically as an only child, I understand what it is to play by myself and get awfully creative. I would pretend that the bushes were my children, or that they were students in a classroom and I was the teacher. This is what we do, we are here to imagine the most outlandish experience possible, but of course it has to be believable even for the creator of the experience, perhaps more so for the creator. It's your game, your hologram. I am part of your hologram and you mine. I need you to be here at this time, and so do you if you are engaged in any aspect of my experience and I in yours.

Let us further examine the importance of our individual creations. Let us first recognize that we can't go "wrong" (*for lack of a better word*) with what we create. You are obviously creating and making choices according to concepts and ideas which would support those decisions. Perhaps in order to create your world five years from now in this moment you will create an experience which will establish an outcome that will influence choices, options, and decisions which will present themselves in the future. It is the way we roll into the next experience. The format of our world has always revolved around themes. Themes represent cycles. The New Age movement represents another theme in a particular period of human evolution/expansion. What happens, however, is due to the nature of our design; we very easily become locked into these patterns and themes. We become comfortable once again with the familiar, this becomes just another programming. Repetition without dimension is programming; where one moves according to a specific set of guidelines without deviation. Such behavior or rituals are also essential in creating discipline, and some guidelines and boundaries, until one feels self-assured enough to hold your own and deviate or add dimension to the disciplines. When one begins to trust him/herself, the guidance unfolds from within. Whatever methods our route we choose is then simply a stepping stone. It is clear that we are privy to and have access to the full spectrum of creation which moves as streams of data. This data takes the shape of the visible world and that which is invisible to us, according to the boundaries placed on one's perception.

It is evident, that in the overall picture, creation does not appear to play it safe otherwise we would have been limited or bridled in the creation of our holograms/private reality. It, however, has a blueprint or patterns of the design to be constructed. Everything is allowed so that we may have the full potential of the human experience. However, for every action there is a reaction. What we create will bear fruit, the vibration of that fruit will determine much of one's experiences. There is no good or bad, there is only the vibration of the reaction. This is what we must contend with, the reaction. Another point to keep in mind is that everything that we do, we do for ourselves. We do it for the payoff; again, this is not a good or a bad thing. I am writing this article because it is helping me to sort through some thoughts and ideas floating around in my mind, as are all my articles and my book. We want to believe that we do it for others, but in truth it is the feeling that is derived from it. Sharing becomes a great outlet. When we do things for our children, or family, or a stranger, it's a great feeling! When we do things that are upsetting to others there is still a payoff; you needed to feel the way you feel after all was said and done. It does not matter what it is, in the end, we do it for ourselves. We get that same feeling when someone else does something that is what we call "shameful", underneath it all we feel elevated as we could not have done that, "we are not that kind of person". How do I know this? Because I have had to examine myself, and to my amazement, I realize the payoff derived from all of it. I could say much about the role of victimization but we will save that for another day. I don't write or share the information because I believe that the world needs saving or that I have the answers, I do because it frees me to be me regardless of the response. It allows me to experience my weaknesses and my strengths, it allows me to stand firmly in my ever-expanding knowing, and if along the way lives are changed because of it then I am ever so grateful for being allowed to be part of one's evolution. My workshops and my lectures allow me the same experience. It is about my growth and that is how I contribute to this beautiful dance I own that it is about me and so I don't have to hide or play it safe in most instances.

Most people play it safe because change is devastating. As I said previously, we each have a model of reality to which we live our lives. When an attitude, people, place, thing, or belief is shifted it becomes a chemical reaction. We are addicted to our lives and it is how it is held together by the chemicals and hormones coursing through us. Shifting anyone of these, even moving a chair, causes adjustments to be made to our hologram, or basically we may have to create a new hologram. This can be scary especially when your entire reality sits on the foundation of your spiritual belief structure and when everything is supported by the other. Who will guide us? What will we do? We are wandering into uncharted territory. Will there be a guide there waiting for me? Who will be there to let me know that I am going the right way? Yes it can be a jolt, but the one thing that I am famous for saying is that "no matter what, you will live, even when you appear to die, you live." Another aspect of thought that can certainly provide support is the realization that you are not running out of time, as time is an essential illusion in order for us to have this linear experience. If there is no spoon; and at heart the universe is but a phantom, then there is no such thing as distance and without the idea of distance there can't be time or gravity for that matter. There is no here nor there, all that exists is this moment and everything else is a speculation. This is where the idea of "time" is formed in the speculation. Another quote from The Holographic Universe by Michael Talbot:

> "Bohm believes the reason subatomic particles are able to remain in contact with one another regardless of the distance separating them is not because they are sending some sort of mysterious signal back and forth, but **because their separateness is an illusion**. He argues that at some deeper level of reality such particles are not individual entities, but are actually extensions of the same fundamental something."

During the writing of the The Holographic Canvas did I know who David Bohm was or Gary Zucave, author of the Dancing Wu li Masters? No I did not, but as I wrote and it was time to form the book my inner guidance directed me to information that would support what I had come to understand on my own. I understood the nature of reality before knowing the words "quantum physics". It was what I asked for, I asked to know from within myself, and to my surprise scientists confirmed this possibility in the above quote. It was necessary to have scientific information to support my own conclusion as it is evident that people are more confident of your claims. On the back of my book The Holographic Canvas it states "like the single cell of a plant our history is encoded in us." We are the single cell and the entire plant all at once! We are streams of data! We are the information itself! We have access to all aspects of knowledge, the question is whether we are in a space to trust that inner knowing or not. We most often must build ourselves up to that space of trust. It is for this reason that every step we take is our pathway leading to endless possibilities. To walk with no boundaries is to no longer fear one's actions, for one has become aware of the significance of the *reaction*. So the question is, do you play it safe or do you go for it?

16

Enough with This "Blissed" Out Agenda!

Ok so I have written about this a number of times but for goodness sakes when I run into this stuff it is so funny...yes it is funny. No I am not laughing at anyone but I am laughing at how creative we are in making this game really exciting! There are a group of new agers that are relentless at overdosing the masses with this construct of a future of bliss, where we hang out with the ascended masters and sing kumbaya all day, while we hug mother earth and just feel nothing but joy and love...oh my god just stop it already!! Oh well maybe you don't have to stop it because I am sure that you will create this medicated psychedelic trip reality for those who prefer not to think. *(You are doing exactly what you need to do)*

Mother earth would actually probably prefer for you to stop trying to "heal the earth"; she knows exactly what to do. Perhaps she would prefer for you to get your s---t together so she will not have to belch everyone off of her chest as we are giving her a bad case of gas and heart burn. It is the common theme for us to want to fix everything and everyone just as long as we don't have to zone in on ourselves and when we do manage to zone in on ourselves we come up with yet another fantasy that makes us special in terms of our contribution on the planet...we become excellent channels and mediums here to bring the message of light and goodwill from third parties. Not a problem someone has to deliver this kind of dream stimulation for those who seek this experience. If this does not apply to you then do not get upset. To know joy is to have known sadness. What if ultimate joy, like peace, is about the balance; swinging neither one way nor the other; no measurement therefore no judgment.

Life is truly a beautiful adventure...all of it! This blissed out agenda infers the necessity of the group mind, the borg agenda in order for everything to go into this "shift" being talked about. I am not even sure if I want to use the word "shift" any more as it has become just another watered down word much like the word "conscious" or "consciousness". There is nothing "right" or "wrong about reality. It just is and each person is "reality happening"; reality in full effect. The individual can however change the course of how reality is playing out for him/her. This choice thing becomes very tricky when we are submerged in stagnant beliefs...who is to say what is stagnant...this is another good question. When I use the word stagnant I am referring to repetitious function without deviation or dimension to it. This of course limits one to seeing only the glass half full if that at all. Such a person is convinced that he/she is bound by the laws of physics as we have been programmed to accept. Contrary to popular belief you are not running out of time...it is not possible! Everything is happing in your experience according to the direction you continue to move in.

As far as the blissed out concept by that I mean the kinds of information instilling the idea that we are all entering the new earth right now and that all your cares and worries will begin to magically go away, the kind of information that encourages seekers to attempt to measures their spiritual progression by aiming to count the "increasing strands of DNA now emerging" in the individual, the kind of information that encourages the belief that we are moving toward the city of light, or that we have a mission to achieve for humanity, or that we are awaiting instructions from the command center or from all of the Ascended Masters and space brothers, that they are waiting in anticipation of our leap into this space of bliss and of course I could go on and on. Yes I know I am a fantasy buster. This all sounds very exciting...a great virtual tour if this is where you are on this journey and you would rather stay asleep then this will be a great vacation/dream for you. No really it does sound like fun! I am not saying that there isn't change in progress, yes there is but it does not mean once again that we are all subject to experiencing the same kind of change! This approach takes one down perhaps a much longer path to self-realization (*this is also ok as you are not running out of time*), how can you become self-realized when everything you are latching on to is external, how can you when every next spiritual move must be confirmed by Archangel Michael or Saint Germain or one of the other "Ascended crew". (*Again continue to do what you need to do*) When exactly does one plan to become sovereign, or perhaps you are planning to go through eternity with them as your guide. I am sure that quite a few of them would love this as some continue to use humanity as power supply; we validate their existence as some are stuck! Much of the channeling reference humanity as kindergartners who need the guidance of these outside forces…this should be your first clue! However those that are perhaps rooting for humanity simply observe our progression without interference because they know that we are them and they are us. We exist on all levels but the majority is challenged in seeing this although they may say it their actions say otherwise. (It is what we should all strive to do; allow others their experience without forcing change upon them or your belief) Therefore all that most will see is that they cannot get by without a savior, they must have their guides and third party instructions from outside forces. (I write my thoughts and share it with others, those who resonate or are curious about what I have to say will read it otherwise no one needs me or anything that I have to say).

Please understand that I am not condemning any of this I am simply pointing out the obvious in the event that one chooses to navigate away from that particular course. I have had emails and phone calls from others who have said to me that "*I am recovering*" (they are recovering) from much of the fluff stuff that had them working overtime to be a "good person" and "love everyone". These people were actually stifling the truth of how they feel, they were afraid of not measuring up. Then they were busy trying to reach their "highest potential" so that they can serve their "true purpose". This kind of belief is immobilizing a great many, it is actually causing them to create new masks from behind, which they operate. Every moment of one's life is leading you through to the next moment of potential and possibilities. You have made no mistakes in your life! Every move you have ever made has been leading you to this moment (that includes being blessed out). To become more dynamic is simply to become more aware of what you have created, what you can create and what you will create in your more aware state. You have always been living your true purpose however you have an opportunity to use the accumulation of knowledge acquired along the way to create from a more conscious state; very aware choices.

Life is by your own design an original design that loops one into program streams with specific experiences and paths until one recognizes the many stages of being a human being. So far what we have become accustomed to is the Stage one/level one sensation of being a human being...oh yes there are many stages but you must learn to love the game not run away from it! As I continue to say the game is beautiful with all its twists and turns. This is science and it will show itself to you according to what you will allow yourself to view as a possibility. Can you see it... how fascinating! What will you choose in this leg of the game...to be blissed out or to get off the spiritual sleeping pills so that you can see more and more of the spectrum! What a rush!

17

Your Bloodline & Collective Storylines

What is your world made of, your personal world? In the resent [recent] workshop *Stop Running from the Matrix*, I presented ideas pertaining to our individual storylines which was quite triggering. For although many had examined the realization of an existence of stories there seem to be a completely new level of realization around the multi-tiered storylines upon which the life of the individual is experienced. There is of course the collective storyline as well; the planetary storyline/s. One such collective storyline currently is *"Health"*. We can currently feel and observe the triggers, the codes stirring all potential latent illnesses within the human gene pool based on bloodlines and ancestral health programs.

Within the United States the trigger has been the Health Care bill. This has been the code activator for illnesses to arise in multiple extremes as people are not only triggered but reminded that they are supposed to get sick. They are reminded of their fragility as a species programmed with a fear of death/annihilation/the possibility of none existence in the game; this becomes the true meaning of the *"human race"*, a literal race. The breast cancer ads remind you to *"race for a cure"*. We are continuously reminded that we have a race to be won against the enemy of *"time"*. The marketing of the "race" has everyone in a spin as much "time/energy" is spent working at escaping or dodging a potential illness. Other triggers have been the race to "fix" the environment and of course more recently there is the oil spill. All around us are triggers to remind us of "health dangers".

What happens next? Well for those who are not "health conscious" as we say then they will subscribe to the marketing of potential illnesses whereby they will see their doctor who will either provide a prescription or recommend a specialist or whatever is essential to assist the individual with bloodline storyline/collective storyline etc. After all you are encoded with memory of the unavoidable patterns of health catastrophes which have occurred throughout what we define as human history. We are lost in a repetition of historic cycles. As for the "health conscious" individual (and I know firsthand) we become pretty much neurotic about our diet. We simply move from one matrix to the next based on the storyline of that matrix. There is the "Raw food matrix" where one feels more protected from potential illnesses caused by cooked food, then there is the vegetarian matrix...with or without dairy products, then there is the fruitarian matrix who says that's all I need to keep me healthy and of course the vegan matrix...no animal products in the diet. In observing my own experience on the wheel I realized just how much time I spent in the store reading the labels for fear of consuming something that I just knew would have an adverse effect on me according to the "heath storyline" I was operating by. What was even more amazing is that the more I eliminated things from my diet was the more I had to eliminate even more things from my diet as I was now fully into my bloodline health story. As I worked at escaping potential health issues like allergies and digestive issues the more I triggered these issues...pretty soon there is not much to eat. At this point you are in hook line and sinker; you are on the "food matrix" trip...jumping from one food matrix to the other...omg! But it does not stop there because the external environment is feeding and supporting this rollercoaster by reminding you of the chemtrails, the poisonous additives to the food, you are reminded of the enzymes and vitamins deficient from the human diet, the damage that can be caused by the sun, the fumes in the air, plastic or paper the dangers of plastic bottles and drinking water. Of course the next fad coming along is one "becoming a breatharian", of course this is generally supported by a disdain for food or it is viewed as a possible straight shoot to enlightenment. (If this happens for you as part of an effortless process great however this does not elevate one above those who are still engaged in the enjoyment of food) We are on a pleasure journey although it does not feel like it. Everything works according the experience sought!

In my book The Holographic Canvas I do speak of the effects of food on the body but what I did not directly mention is the storylines attached to the individual. Well one might say what about a baby; well a baby is still a being occupying an earth vehicle. As a being this baby's vehicle/body has the codes/programs and storylines of his/her bloodline. These health codes/programs/stories are activated according to what is required for the journey so is it really about the food or does the food simply serve the storyline being activated. The food/health movement presents and supports a series of storylines as food is so nurturing and healing to our emotional state. So what role does our emotional state play in the food game? isn't our emotional state attached to some sort of storyline regardless of what we do. Everything about our life is fueled by a layer of conditions stemming from our bloodline as well as the collective story; from here we create scripts for our individual stories. We nurture and coddle everything about our experiences including our health. It's an opportunity to build a segment in one's life around health conditions or concerns. Just think about how involved you become in any condition that you are told you have or that you believe you are dealing with. This is not a good or a bad thing as it is simply part of a segment of the experiences one has added to ones adventure in what we define as *"your life"*. The "matrix of food storylines" however provides one with enough supporting content in traveling through the food/health matrix. We become part of the movement; a movement that becomes just another religion to which one chooses a food matrix within which one can play his/her role with all the content that will be provided by similar players.

In the event that one feels the need to defend ones diet there is no need to, you are doing exactly what is needed for your story just as I have (I have however gotten off that wheel). You are nurturing your script as any great performer should. You must make the role believable to yourself otherwise you will not gain the treasure from the outcome. The coding is already in your genes/bloodline waiting for the right opportunity to be triggered into a full blown story! Yes now we have something to work with! Childhood trauma, relationship trauma, failure, rejection or ones embrace of the patterns of health issues associated with one's bloodline are all silent triggers. One must now work at escaping or *"run for a cure"*. In teaching lymphology in the past, I have always told the class that they eat for two objectives, pleasure and fuel. So exactly what is the body converting into energy from earth produced foods? that would be trapped sunlight from the food. We are eating sunlight. However one may eat meat and receive the essentials for his/her body based on the health storyline (everything is alive whether it be flesh or plants, everything is in agreement of this experience, we eat bugs day in and day out each time we open our mouths or breath). In the end it is the evolution of one's consciousness that is determining the condition of the body. Consciousness represents levels of self-awareness; it represents both the expansiveness of one's awareness as well as the limitations of one's awareness. In the even bigger picture, all of the conditions of our environment being imposed on our "health" can be overridden in the body as the energy from the storylines are drained and put to rest. This is not about positive thinking this is about a deep realization of our individual game that we have been caught in and ending it. There is a hidden fear for many should these *stories* story no longer be there…then what next…what will you do? Those stories and conditions have been our motivation for living so to speak. "Those stories filled up my life, what will I focus on if I no longer have to be imprisoned by the environment and the food matrix? What will become of me when there are no stories to swap?"

If ones profession involves supporting the health storyline, do not be despondent, as We are all helping each other support our storyline in one form or another. What I would say is to become aware of the story that you may tell yourself that people need fixing

auk

but instead go ahead and embrace the role you play as just that a role. This is what your hologram called for. As I have often said no body needs me however I am receptive to a particular game experience when it's presented. Once we begin to let go of the exasperating assessment of potential demise to the body or our overall existence we will regain tremendous power and a sense of wholeness instead of feeling like a captive of our story. There is so much more beyond the realm of focus which we have committed to the physical experience. Sight becomes less and less impeded by the distraction of the struggle to preserve oneself in the physical existence. The less that one struggles to maintain the body based on physical remedies and instead elevate the body into the field of timelessness the body will no longer be forced to function in fragmentation, defending itself against this thing or that thing as there is no this thing or that thing simply an illusion of segments; a beautiful illusion that continues to allow us the most amazingly believable experience in what seems to be an eternity but is only a moment. We must now give our bodies permission to operate without these fractured experiences in realizing that the body takes its cue from our belief systems and hidden storylines. So can we change course? Sure we can, will it be challenging? More than likely, yes. Remember that as you choose to change course that which you have worked at escaping might seem to emerge but the key is to remind yourself that you cannot be fooled by your eyes. The thoughts will come in association with the old storylines and genetic/bloodline programs but you do not have to sign up for it and over time you will find that your over assessment which generally triggers these storylines no longer emerge. Instead you simply act according to an immediate connection with the inner more expansive self. Then there is nothing to fear and you are now ready for a more expansive experience in the field of possibilities.

18

Who's In Charge of the Human's?

This is a question that is well worth examining from many different angles. Who is in charge of the humans, do humans need handlers/controllers? Humans are hardwired to be controlled; hard wired for slavery. Because of this the vast majority readily accept the need for control by government, corporations, religion/spiritual constructs and education. These systems are presented to us from birth as separate forces through which our lives are subtly restricted and controlled.

It is clear that this kind of hard wiring convinces us to relinquish our power to those who have hypnotized us into believing that they know what is best for us. Guidance from our parents is certainly essential upon entering this realm of forgetfulness. However the above systems of control have acted as an extension of the guidance of our parents. Reality as experienced from its more basic and common levels is a unique *cult* experience (yes I said cult experience) as we sway to subtle tones of conformity. We cling dearly to common actions, common possibilities and common results. Even our scientists struggle with pushing the envelope and there are those who have suffered great ridicule or worse for birthing new possibilities although not yet proven. (Unless of course such discoveries can be used to more easily enslave). *"Cultures"* are models of a much vaster cult experience. Within any culture there are prototypes or standards by which this "cultural system" will operate. It therefore challenges a mind born, raised and shaped completely by one culture or ideal in functioning in newly introduced cultures. Our brains are wired to the hologram of cultural norms and acceptability's. It is for this reason that we are wired to fight and to defend the nerve center of our hologram, which for many is the culture, associated with their land or community. Humans are all about timing as we appear to be on cyclic timers determining the surge of new concepts and ideas which will emerge with gradual acceptance at first by a few and eventually by all. We are on the brink of a massive technological upsurge. This coincides with the much-emphasized Mayan prophecies centered on the year 2012 and that which comes afterwards.

We have been taught to honor the cycles as our ancestors have but it's evident that unless we can connect with planetary history some million years ago we will continue to run into dead ends leading us back to a reconfigured concept of earth. I am speaking of frequencies, which create a distinct field of limited experiences for a human being. We are operating in a field of tones, which assist in rendering levels of the brain inaccessible. Just as we can only see colors within the scope of the field created for us to operate within, when we listen to certain kinds of music which is elevating to the spirit and to the brain we are only hearing and experiencing a limited scope of the dimensions of those tones; the frequencies of those tones. Keep in mind that this is all within the expression of the game. The purpose of such observation is to stimulate the mind beyond this isolated and captivating playing field held together by our own minds. The cycles determine a potential collective shift in humans becoming increasingly self-aware or as we say an evolution in consciousness. This acceptance is widespread as much is heard about the shift in consciousness for the planet. So should one honestly examine these observations you will realize precisely what I have expressed. We are excited about the possibility of experiencing something new other than the feeling of spiritual and physical helplessness so we delight in the possibility of the ending and beginning of a new cycle. But can we stop for a moment to examine the nature of the wheel that we have rendered ourselves powerless to? It's as if humanity is caught on a hamster wheel. Most of our observation is centered on the general movement of the cosmic system. Yes examine that word carefully, *"system"*. Our consciousness is wired to a timed cosmic system. Wikipedia: *"The term system may also refer to a set of rules that governs behavior or structure"*.

Atlantis is a system program, a code strongly responsible for the energy field of intercepting tones which ensure the imprisonment of the mind in this field of limitation. Is this farfetched? No because those kinds of experiments are being carried out by humans on the planet at this time. This is the age of technological advancements. The question is were these cycles orchestrated and preset to impact the human wiring, the human programming, the brain, the mind based on a specific time, of course "time" as determined by the number of cycles in rotation. A specific response is triggered by the ending and beginning of each period; simply another experiment within the human game. The entire cosmic system within which we are confined appears to be intricately designed and upon contact with the harmonics (hormones/chemicals) of the human vehicle, a psychedelic experience is triggered presenting us with a pre-recorded construct of the reality we are now addicted to. However due to unique chemical signatures each being is able to construct his/her own version of reality who's core foundation will always be rooted in the general cosmic system coding. To better understand the movement of the cyclic process and its impact on our lives here is a quote from a three part workshop I did in February 2010 titled *Hacking the Mind & breaking Reality Code* (the full 7 hours is available for download or CD & DVD);

"The concept of a Human being is a program setup to allow the existence of the life of human beings to run/live for a predestined number of cycles, regulated by the moon.

Although most people are aware of the passing of cycles and their general effect on human life they are not aware of the true nature of the boundaries set by these cycles. We are not aware of a programmed confinement to the general blueprint or program. The most obvious cyclic regulators from our limited vision are the sun and the moon. These cycle regulators are streaming the programs based on the blueprint or program. Our bodies are dependent on the sun and the moon. They completely regulate our sleeping and waking cycles. They regulate chemical transitions such as the synthesizing of the neurotransmitters serotonin and melatonin. The daylight brings us Serotonin and the night time brings us melatonin. The brain responds to the light change. These cycles put us to bed and they wake us up. They also keep track of our life cycle more specifically the moon. You may wander as I did how it is that the body knows to start puberty after so many cycles or birthdays, how does the body know to start shutting you down. The individual cycles are determined by the planetary alignment at the time of the birth of each program/human, each program is generated intentionally based on a particular zodiacal cycle according to the history of the program stream associated with the **genetic lineage** through which the individual (program) will emerge along the history stored in the holographic record keeper called the soul.

Our bodies are tied into the calendar cycles based on the movement of the planet based on the moon cycle and the impact of all other planets in our orbit, solar system, the entire scape/landscape backdrop seen and unseen it's all a programmed reality relating to our experience as a human being. The universes as we know it is a holographic system within which all of its components are then holographic. The hologram is a program. Everything is moving and tied into the cycles of this holographic machine. It's a dreamscape. To participate in the experience of this holographic dream world without losing sight of one's memory one must become a conscious animator of one's vehicle/body and dream experience. What I have come to realize even more profoundly is the manner in which our entire physical experience is programmed into to this holographic experience, as I indicated before **we are a program-a running program in the program of the hologram**, we are running programs."

So let's take it a step further. Let's examine this vast playground of beings centered around the game of earth. Is it possible that this shift is really about the dying away of gurus, guides, saviors and our old concepts of ascended masters. Is it possible that there is a struggle to keep the general populous from awakening to the fact they are no longer needed. What if this is a window of opportunity that will remove the veil for a brief moment for those who are open to seeing the illusion of the game and the hypnotizers of humanity; those who wired humans with the savior program and the external god program. When you examine the Lord Maitreya movement, they have constructed an entire school based on the opportunity for students to step up and assume various cosmic offices not unlike the office of the Christ held by Lord Maitreya, Sanat Kumara or as overseers of the planet. There is also the office of the "god" of the planet. Everyone wants to be in charge of earth. Now all of these beings report back to a "god" so the question is, who is it that they report to? There is an actual distinctly advanced force to which they report and it is their job to bring everyone else, such as us, into the fold of this specific force. Here we have the light workers. They have been brought into the light as defined by the masters who rule what level/aspect of light they are dealing with. One may say that this is utter nonsense and another may be quite on board for this. Now I heard such comments as "this is just ridiculous as Jesus is the true light of the world and he is coming back", I have also heard this is correct because St Germain said so, or Archangel Michael said so. Well what do you say? You are equally as great as all these forces presented to you. The psychology of this kind of brain washing is staggering yet it can be seen in all of our daily lives.

There has been quite a number done on the human mind in programming an acceptance of feebleness and an inaccessibility to the sovereign power source which is you! I am sure that there will be comments which state that "since they are still us what does it matter" well you are correct it does not matter at least not to you but for those of you like myself who would prefer to peel away the costumes and throw away the crutch behind which your worthiness is hidden as we limp along in the game then it matters. IT IS A GAME! Games are to be played and figured out! In this level of the game we have the opportunity to go beyond this limited aspect of the game but one cannot do so unless we allow ourselves to see the humor of the game and the amazing master players who continue to assist us to hold on to the deception. You begin to ask questions like why are we so minimally encouraged to tap into ourselves without these third parties who continue to refer to us as "Dear Ones" or "little ones" basically? The majority of these handlers are males! How lopsided is this! There is no balance in gender frequency/vibration. This is a giant male frequency dominated game through and through! The focus here is from an energy perspective so please set aside anatomy or anatomic value. The male and female genders are like everything else all vibration based; it is about the charge that each holds or represents; a positive and a negative charge. Although we each hold both frequencies in these bodies one frequency becomes the primary frequency which the individual will re-present in the game; a male or female charge. This entire process should indeed raise a red flag, but due to our programming of acceptability, there is minimal questioning or such concerns are subtly validated. Most of the vessels for such communication are women however, which lends a certain level of camouflage or distraction away from the obvious. On a deeper note this is the design/construct of the game experience so again I am only pointing out these trappings of the game only if one is open to viewing further down the rabbit hole and if you are not, great! This is without a doubt a fascinating game. To delve more deeply into much of this information you may view my other article titled *Government of the Matrix.*

To continue an examination into the self-appointed offices and officers of the planet below is a quote from Dr. Joseph David Stone a supporter and student of Lord Maitreya:

"To begin with, the "Office of the Christ" on a planetary level is an inner plane Spiritual governmental position that Lord Maitreya has held for over 2000 years! He took over this position even prior to the Master Jesus' sojourn on Earth! It was Lord Maitreya, the Planetary Christ, who over lighted Jesus, along with the Christ, the second aspect of the Trinity. A great many of the famous quotes of Jesus were actually channelings Jesus was doing of Lord Maitreya and the Christ, which is why they are so profound! Lord Maitreya, as the current Planetary Christ, is the President of the Planet and is the Head of the Spiritual Hierarchy. On the planetary level he also holds an overlighting synthesis Spiritual leadership of the Seven Chohans and the Seven Ray departments. He and the Manu Allah Gobi, and the Mahachohan/Saint Germain along with Lord Buddha the Planetary Logos are given a certain structure or grid of the Divine Plan from Helios and Vesta, our Solar Logos, and it is their job to fill in their squares so to speak with all their Spiritual battleplans along with the Seven Chohans and the leader of the inner plane Synthesis Ashram.

The Spiritual leadership of the inner plane Synthesis Ashram was passed on to me by the inner plane Ascended Master Djwhal Khul, who has left for his next cosmic position at the Great White Lodge on Sirius but still works with the Earth as well! The inner plane Synthesis Ashram is a miniaturized Office of the Christ, which is part of my attunement to Lord Maitreya, and the Office of the Christ!

It is the purpose of the Office of the Christ to create integrated Planetary Christs and/or 12th to 22nd degree initiates and Masters. This is done through Spiritual education through a Seven Ray synthesis approach! Lord Maitreya, Allah Gobi the Manu, and Saint Germain the Mahachohan form a Trinity, just as God, Christ and the Holy Spirit is a Trinity!"

Again you may call this entire thing crazy but if it's so crazy then why is the United Nations so involved in supporting the Lord Maitreya's movement. I will not cover it in the scope of this article as it would be a very lengthy article but I will say this there is a great fear of humanity discovering that we have been operating under this deceptive spiritual umbrella. This is the tie in with pretty much all spiritual organizations. They all have an individual force to which they hold allegiance. For humans to discover the freedom to be a sovereign force that recognizes that he/she is creation in a profound way without the need for the crutch of worshipping outside of him/herself, this would affect the current construct of the game. I believe that it is clear that very few will shift beyond that leg of reasoning in the game at least in this moment of time as we are experiencing it. I also do not believe that everyone is to awaken to that realization. We are all walking into the experiences needed along the way and some humans require this kind of illusory leadership in fulfilling the outline of their game experience in this realm. After all we are all in this cosmic game system for the sheer joy of the experience, from planetary god to Ascended Master to limited human. We are engaged in the game of ruler and subject. Those things that are shared here in this article or in any of my other writings are for those who find a resonance with it. For some there is a tugging and a deep yearning to pierce the bubble, which one may feel confined to. Sometimes you get glimpses beyond the bubble, a quick image that shows you that there are options of a more vast life not beholden to the rulers of the planet. Although reality exists in a paradox of real and unreal within those moments of interaction and feedback we are involved in process of the game in whatever way that may be. Now lest I be chastised I am not saying that all communicative beings are out to get us. There are many who wish us well and do hope that we are able to see beyond the smoke and mirrors of a cosmic game and game players who have been at it for quite some time.

Do I feel as if I need to fix anything? No! Do I feel as if the world needs to be saved? No! Do I need to shout about the Sacred Feminine? No! The only thing that I need to do is to simply be and to embrace the knowingness that I am that which I seek. Where ever you are in your role-playing at this time is an experience to be acknowledged and appreciated, for in any given moment that experience may cease to be and new possibilities will perhaps be embraced. We are profound beings in an a-maze-ing adventure of self-discovery! Go beyond the light where there is no light only nothingness and from there we create just as we have this mind boggling experience we call life!

19

The Marketing of "Reality" & The Universal Corporation
A Cosmic Empire

The strategic marketing of reality serves as the model from which marketing concepts, network marketing, the stock market, sales strategies and our corporate, government and political structure is derived. As is often said "as above so below" this applies in all facets of movement on the physical plane. Reality as collectively perceived is marketed to our psyche, and projected through neural simulation.

THE HIERARCHICAL STRUCTURE-MANY LEVELS OF CREATORS

There is no doubt a hierarchical system in place. A few of these levels are the gravitationally bound humans, the transforming human, beings unrestricted by the physics of the third dimension, overseers of humanity in the third dimension, masters of time, creators of worlds/galaxies, those beyond the confines of thought or definition.

It is important to keep in mind that there is a progressive structure in place operating in layers above this familiar concept of reality I am referring to that of the gravitationally bound human. Each descending level is governed by the preceding level yet all levels are ultimately impacting the other.

We have bought into a concept and signed a contract with the experience. Religious and spiritual organizations are the best at marketing and recruiting new buyers, new customers. If we are able to examine reality as projected or as accepted we can begin to see a dynamic corporatized system.

CORPORATION Definition: *"As to define a corporation in business language, it is body with its own lawful characters distinct from its stockholders or owners. Due to this instance, the law provides it with its own legal rights and responsibilities. A corporation then has the right to charge and be charged in court. It may retain properties and assets separate from its members. It may also recruit employees who can help in operating the business. More so, a corporation may engage in contracts and agreements with other entities. And, it may set and implement its own by-laws that will regulate and control its internal dealings."*

In this reference I am not speaking of the lower level 3D corporate structure driven by commerce. However commerce serves as a tool of control as we are navigated through this *timeshare marketing* experience. Our experience on earth as we know earth to be is very much like buying timeshare in a virtual world. The marketing of reality is as relentless as McDonalds marketing strategies. McDonalds realizes that in order to keep their current customers and continue to recruit new ones they can never take a break from running commercials. It is important that McDonald's logo remains an imprint in all its new and old cult members/customers.

All organizations are held together by the same model; a hierarchical system which of course spells out rank, importance, seniority, power status, or authority. Our position on the game board of earth's (earth as more commonly experienced) reality is taking place based on this hierarchical system, however illusionary. The focus point of the marketing of reality from its limiting approach, serves to ensure the sale of externalizing concepts to participants.

It is clear that in all structures (as woven into our psyche) someone at the top must always rule those at the bottom or those on the next level down. So is it coincidence that we operate our world in this manner; it's been driven home into our minds, our cells and our DNA that someone must always rule. Such a structure defines the corporatizing concept, from slaves to the slave owner and above the owner is the marketing team, the go betweens and above them is the generator of the idea or concept builder. This idea has been driven home so strongly that we are completely convinced that we cannot rule ourselves. At this stage of the game self-rulership is not for everyone yet on a profound level of existence we have given permission for this experience. This article is about an examination of the game experience from those angles where we have been shut out or from which we have shut ourselves out. There is no doubt a multileveled game at work. To understand it from its scientific movements by exploring its illusory subatomic components and beyond; is to see only the technology of the fabrication of existence/reality etc. In other words to view it only from the level of the mechanical movement of energy will alter or limit more in depth insight into that which moves the wheel. Yes we know that it is consciousness but there is still a degree of clarity that is untapped in regards to consciousness. We are consciousness systems yet this is still not the core essence of who we are. The mechanism of consciousness serves to allow the nothingness to investigate all that it could potentially be otherwise nothingness need not discover itself. It could not play with itself. It is the sound of one hand clapping. (This was discussed in the three-part workshop Hacking the Mind and Breaking Reality Codes) Again will we ever get to the core of who we are? The only time that we do is when we are "nothing". So the intricate layering of existence in its corporate game format and its hierarchical systems work in unison with the unending big bang and the contracting and releasing process which turns the wheel of possibilities in that which we call our universe and beyond that; all computised systems within systems.

In any game there must be an objective, the origin of that objective has to be initiated by a creator. Those concepts are born from the mind of the imaginer. The creator of the game knows much more about the possibilities and potentials of the game although not yet experienced so the best way to bring the game to life is to incorporate players. Players are positioned according to the extent of their knowledge of the game, some watch and learn, some monitor the game, and some incorporate strategies to establish more complexity or challenges in the game. As players become engrossed in the game their focus becomes locked into maneuvering through their position in the game. Although they may have started out with an awareness that the overall objective is to ascend to levels of full awareness of the game, whereby establishing him/herself as a game creator; a conscious game creator; this is soon forgotten. We must keep in mind that full awareness of the game in this context is simply the achievement of **mastery over matter**. This is something that we do not emphasize as we are programmed to accept that it is only for those we regard as chosen or powerful beings. Not so! To master death is to master matter. It is the reason for this quietly kept secret for we would join the ranks of great cosmic magicians. This biblical reference from the book of Corinthians is significant *"The last enemy that shall be destroyed is death.* We all know that there is much coded information in the bible. Another important reference *"Ye are gods"* Psalm 82:6. Players are distracted Alchemists.

So here we can begin to see the manner in which the configuration of the game becomes a giant corporate structure. As the game branched off into the imagined and the unimagined forming various levels each level developed its own uniqueness although still a component of the overall game. The game became a winding staircase of levels of achievements spiraling upwards; a staircase of unfolding knowledge leading to the originator of the game. These concepts can be seen in all organizational structures. It is the reason competition is such an essential component in our experience. Competition drives us to the prize whatever the prize maybe to us in that moment. These ball games, teams and fans are a great example of our delight in the game experience. An entire team is owned by someone, but each owned player has agreed to this, they have signed a contract for the payoff, for the promised or agreed on compensation, or the player has the option of being an independent player, making his/her own choices still yet limited by boundaries.

The overall game experience forms the invisible corporation, structured uniquely to fulfill an agenda; from the gaseous laws of this environment to these physical bodies designed suitably for the agenda. The system however branches off into subdivisions to accommodate the various stages of progression of the expanding reality; the players/characters/employees/rulers and subjects within it. All throughout history stories are recorded or passed down of various enlightened beings coming at the end and at the beginning of new cycles. So what's going on here…well were they just making this up? No, as I pointed out previously there is a system in place, there are stages to this game with subdivisions and beings/players positioned in these various stages as part of the navigation system of the game. The planets and various star systems in place are all part of a rotation mechanism which supports the agenda of the larger game; after all these systems are created by creators who are on the level of being aware creators.

Such components as angels, guides, and archangels are part of the management simulation program routed through the nervous system. They are in place to support the awakening or hypnotized/sleeping player making his/her way through the game or up the ladder of knowledge. There is a point of play where they are no longer an essential component, but you decide when they are no longer necessary to your game experience. We begin to realize that we have been a franchise of the greater model of reality; the hologram from which we have built our own holographic franchise. A franchise is recognized by its logos, symbols, practices and modeled concept. What is franchising?

Franchising is the practice of using another firm's successful business model. The word 'franchise' is of anglo-french derivation - from franc- meaning free, and is used both as a noun and as a (transitive) verb.[1][2]

For the franchisor, the franchise is an alternative to building 'chain stores' to distribute goods and avoid investment and liability over a chain. The franchisor's success is the success of the franchisees. The franchisee is said to have a greater incentive than a direct employee because he or she has a direct stake in the business.

However, it must be noted that, except in the US, and now in China (2007) where there are explicit Federal (and in the US, State) laws covering franchise, most of the world recognizes 'franchise' but rarely makes legal provisions for it. Only France and Brazil have significant Disclosure laws but Brazil regulates franchises more closely.

Where there is no specific law, franchise is considered a distribution system, whose laws apply, with the trademark (of the franchise system) covered by specific covenants. http://en.wikipedia.org/wiki/Franchising

Once we become aware of this course of movement we begin stirring to understand more about our storylines and the imbalances in one's experience. Imbalance in no way implies that your experiences are right or wrong, good or bad but simply questioned experiences by you. Understanding that the management program is written into our neural system or nervous system more easily explains why we readily fall in line with the search for a savior or some sort of managing force. Now for many it is very hard to imagine a perception no longer based on a management team, after all this acceptance is as essential as breathing air for most of us. A side effect of the management simulation/ program is the subservience and surrender to the relinquishment of power. Yet our need for support and rescue is understandable. Between the complexities and the challenges endured in human experience, combined with our lack of memory; one is forced to embrace the anticipated rescue implied by the management simulation/ program.

In an excerpt from my book The Holographic Canvas *"The power of ever expanding knowledge is profound as it generates spiritual fire* mystical *in the human brain, stimulating the production of dormant chemicals within the limbic system. The Limbic system-also known to the Taoist as **crystal***

Crystal Palace

palace- includes: *the Pineal gland, Hypothalamus, Pituitary and the Thalamus. This area of the brain plays a key role in storage of memories of our life experiences and also maintains chemical balance. As we reunite with this understanding we will begin to release the programming associated with aging as the brain is introduced to a continuous resurgence of energy. Knowledge of such magnitude will take us beyond the sustenance required by a mortal existence. Time and space, as known; becomes almost obsolete as we discover the infiniteness of mind"*, this clearly examines the mechanisms responsible for accessing other states of consciousness or better yet the board room or various levels of stored knowledge fundamental in returning to full awareness of the game. In an interview with Frank Joseph, Author of Opening the Ark of the Covenant he talked about the effect of the electrical discharge from the Ark on the hippocampus in the brain. His research indicated that the impact on the hippocampus from the negative ions from the Ark (the sacred stone/crystal within the Ark) allowed altered states of consciousness. In these altered states of consciousness the individual had the experience of being in the presence of godly beings. Of course this was seen as an enlightening experience for the individual. The beings seen and the experience had directly correlate and reflect the deity worshipped in the individual's spiritual practice. Notice that we all must be part of a ritual of worship; you must belong to a "fate"; you must have a belief system in place, generally you are born into one although you may convert to another later on in your life. What is also interesting to note is that although one may not actively practice, when one is asked about their religious club the response might be things like "well I was raised catholic" or "well I am catholic" or "I was raised Christian" or a number of other responses. My point is not to criticize but to point out the spiritual categorization that we are conditioned into.

So getting back to the altered states experienced under the influence of the Ark, because our desire is so strong to be next to god or to experience these encoded concepts of what god is, very little questioning is asked by most. This kind of altered experience then

Ark- what is it?

happens

supports ones religious belief. Worship of course becomes even more heightened towards those beings as one has experienced proof of your god's existence. Let's examine the modern equivalence. This can be seen with the rise of channeling as the audience is magnetized towards the experience of communicating with one who is evidently occupying an altered state; another realm let's say. Again I am not judging the experience, as all experiences are valid otherwise we would not have them.

Another interesting experience with the Ark was that any nation possessing the Ark (the stone/crystal) historically has experienced a Golden Age as progress and an enlightened sense of being flourished over the land in every way imaginable. However a side effect of having the Ark removed was a debilitating collapse of that nation. They were more severely crippled than before they had the Ark. Individuals in possession of the Ark experienced much the same thing or an increase in thirst for power. Technology like this is without a doubt a real setup in the game. Although according to Frank Joseph research has not yet pinned down the creator of the Ark.

The developing, or at least the concept of this un-datable mechanism no doubt descended from higher levels of the game. The power of the Ark is still woven into our world today. The stage one human in this limiting leg of the game; the worker is responding as required in this level of the system. Just as long as the worker/player continues to hang on to promises of a promotion to higher enlightenment in heaven ones franchise/hologram will continue to model the limiting franchise purchased. But the journey to enlightenment is a game and sometimes the overdose of seriousness becomes the pitfall as views become one-dimensional. It's the peripheral vision that is powerful, it's the shadows caught out the corner of the eye...now there is magic there for much of what is caught by direct visual experience is limiting and preprogrammed. Remember that our contact with the physical world is based on our library of familiarities and acceptability's in the brain and those familiarities are supported by our belief systems and perceptions.

The business of reality when summed up is equivalent to the business model of our world. In the business of reality the commercial mode of exchange is spiritual currency. We are spending our energy; our life force as allotted in the illusion of a finite existence. We operate from an illusory space of spending time; time is the means of calculating or measuring spiritual currency; your life force or so we are lead to believe in the game. In our world of commerce currency is based on instruments designated/agreed on as the mode of exchange. The science of currency/commerce ideally requires such instruments of exchange to be backed by a natural/tangible substance such as gold or silver. When we allow ourselves to see beyond the accepted norm we will see clues are all around us. When we speak about god (and this includes those who consider themselves aware) we do so with a sense of externalization; acknowledged as a force outside and separate from us. I have witnessed this despite religious/spiritual beliefs. This is a programming/conditioning that is deeply embedded in most everyone. We want to meet god and *do his will,* this is what is said by many, but whose will and which god? The fact is that there is a god/creator for this and all other worlds. So our desire to connect with a force seen as separate is not completely without merit. These are highly aware beings! This realization is significant in becoming aware of the human potential to rise or to return to such levels of being a "conscious creator". This is what is possible for each of us! If we are at all serious about a deep stimulation of memory we must be willing to examine our spiritual belief systems beyond the euphoric comfort zone. A franchise owner can someday choose to create his/her own company completely unrelated to the franchise previous owned. However the skills learned from operating the franchise has prepared one to build a magnificent empire; a world of unique ideas inspired by the highs and lows of the previous experiences. In ones new world/empire one will incorporate workers/characters/

franchisees/players/ a team of upper and lower management to fulfill that which has been imagined and so the cycle repeats itself as we hit the agenda point of the game/corporation/business.

Technology is the medium of conversion of substance (energy let's say) into formation. It is the mechanism of creating on all levels. Technology redefines itself according to the level or realm of creative capability. All creators operate through inner technology regardless of one's level of awareness. There are some base principles in manifesting ideas and concepts from the depth of the imagination. Even in creating one's own enslavement. So the levels of technology understood in our realm are a stepping stone to more advanced levels of a greater technology in use by beings who have governed this enterprise of earth. We hear of corporate take over's and we have also heard many stories of the scuffle for the control of earth by external forces. Is it any different? No. It takes me back to my article WHO IS IN CHARGE OF THE HUMANS? Our entire universe is a giant enterprise run by a multileveled hierarchical governing systems. As I have said in other articles this entire process is a virtual program. At heightened levels the technology changes to functions and possibilities generated by inner technology of advanced gods/administrators/board members. We can also identify them as high ranking cosmic scientists. Now let's put things in perspective comparatively in observation of our scientific community on this level of the game, can you see the parallel...as above so below. We are attempting to remember and to replicate the very system that we have been playing in or perhaps appear to be trapped in, (in terms of being trapped this depends on your perspective of course). On this level of the game it's as if we are building a time machine from scrap metal or from materials accessible on this realm, however on other levels their technology requires no materials to be gathered only the actions of mere thought. Such beings are the forces that we pay homage to the forces that we worship. To put things further in perspective, let's compares our position to a third world country or fourth world country measured against a first world system. Let us keep in mind that every country is a business, every city, and every town all run and owned by governing systems. Although at the core of it all the people are generally the rightful owners, the people most often give away their rights to others who they believe to be more capable of making decisions on their behalf and almost always the people (the real owners) are made the workers. The entire world is a giant corporation with a handful of ruling forces who answer to these hierarchical systems previously mentioned. This becomes significant in viewing the deceptions imposed in the area of spirituality. Spirituality is corporatized and only a select few are deemed privy to selected levels of knowledge. When we sell out or when we bargain with our personal evolution that which we have bargained with or sold out to holds all the cards. It might be quite a few life times before one wises up to the boundaries and the manipulation written into the contract signed. But as always I must say that time is an illusion so nothing has been lost, no one is running out of time, this is all part of the mechanism that keeps the wheel turning and the universal corporation going.

The beauty lies in the awakening to the agenda and in remembering profound levels of capabilities and possibilities in human expansion. When we can recognize the boundaries and the limitations gated around our perceptions only then will the veil thin away into none existence at least in this realm of the game experience, when we are no longer afraid to live a life without the mindset of subservience only then are we ready to assume the power that lies within us waiting ever so patiently to be unleashed. This kind of power is for everyone <u>but</u> at different stages of expansion. Therefore it is not for everyone to experience complete disclosure or awakening on the level of the experience just as we are all on different levels of awareness. Evolution is personal and we must realize that who you are and your desire for deep evolution is not contingent on the whole world shifting. However your personal transformation will create a world within which you can and will continue your progression. You don't have to beg the world to change, just you, you are the only one that needs to change; change your perception and your relationship with the world will change. This vast business you operate in will adjust, adapt and reform according to your new perception of reality. The universal hierarchy at every level has its own dilemmas that it must contend with so perhaps in realizing this we can set aside our ideology of perfection. All beings are in constant evolution; this game is about endlessly creating and with creating comes endless progression. Perhaps we should redefine the idea of creating, as all potentials exist in the ocean of possibilities. We cast images or bring into form models of all such potentials and possibilities. With such awareness it is clear that we endlessly rediscover the fullness of who and what we are in those moments where we pulse into nothingness, no particle, no wave just abundant nothingness and when the pulse reappears we return to the game. This article is meant to stimulate more thought and if otherwise interpreted then it has still stimulated more thought. In the end the shape of your reality is truly in your hands!

20

2010... A New Linear Cycle Spun by Ancient Technology

We are indeed embarking on a new cycle. A new cycle called 2010. It is the entrance into what is recognized as "a New Year". Each new year; new cycle is the result of the culmination of all prior cycles. Cycles are segmented periods between two points...which we recognize as "time"; having a beginning and an end. It is within these two points that we experience our own cycles. Are we affected by the general cycle defined by the period known as a "year"? Yes indeed...why? Because we are wired into the cycles of the turning wheel. Each cycle has its own theme; its own guidelines, its own rules by which the collective human experience is mapped. Simply put there are some base guidelines for operating in this system. The question is, are we confined to the motion of this wheel; are we tied to the movement and the conditions of this wheel; this blueprint. No! However it is an essential guideline for the navigation of the dreaming human; it is an integral part of the game. It is a fundamental technology set in place for the navigation of the entire human experience.

We speak of ancient engineers and architects but never do we speak of programmers. As humans we fear the thought of a drop in the "value" principles which we have placed on ourselves as humans. The thought of accepting the realization that we operate in these uniquely engineered vehicles scares most as there is that sense of losing value. To become aware of such truths will actually open one up to the "observer" that you are, as you are only driven around in your body/vehicle. There is a great technology at work and it is from this technology that we build our computers and our machineries. We speak of the Mayan Calendar and the calculations done by indigenous groups on the planet including the Sumerians and the Dogons, they speak of cycles. They speak of Gods, they speak of those from the Sky, but what and who are these forces that seem to enter this virtual world? Yes our virtual reality. How is the "space" called reality truly being run, what is the cosmic technology behind it. Do you want to know or are you simply satisfied with the fact that you were engineered by another set of beings? What is it that was engineered, was it simply the vehicle/body? Most certainly...as consciousness cannot be engineered however the mind connected with the vesicle [vehicle] can be overshadowed or blocked due to the design of the vehicle/body. One might say well if it is only the body that has been engineered then why can't I simply jump into a greater awareness? Well there is difficulty as humans have convinced themselves that they are completely their body. So all that is accessed is the programming of the body, which is genius in terms of the extensive data that it holds and from which it runs itself.

The body is then wired into the cycles which produce the concept we view as "linear time". How is time "generated" in this turning wheel? An essential question that should be asked by those who are ready to step outside of their human programming for just a moment so that you can see more of the intricacies of this dream world you are in. Amazing, amazing, amazing! Scientists and others will tell you that you can't see it but I am here to tell you that you can see it once you can step outside of your program, not just your individual program but the collective human program. I will say this to you the current program being offered by this unfolding cycle is one of the "group mind" concept disguised as the "enlightenment" idea of merging into "oneness". There is oneness always but not necessarily a complete integration, which would set aside the individualized aspect of core consciousness. This individualized aspect as imagined by core consciousness is essential in the movement of its imagination through all of its potentials. Now will there be some who will participate in this Borg consciousness? Most definitely! Remember that the potentials and possibilities are endless. You are part of a vast imagination machine. Is your fate sealed to move in this direction? No! Each of us is the face of "core consciousness", we are each paradoxically core consciousness. Many would have you sign on for the "no choice" rule. Choice however is an intricate science as all choices being made by the dreaming human is tied to a vast stream of inherited codes and programs from which we each operate. The idea of being an awakened being requires so much more that the illusion by which many so termed "conscious people" are willing to explore. Well you might say, Sonia do you consider yourself to be an awakened being…well I will say this, I have discovered a great many truths and continue to discover and awaken to knowledge that reminds me of just how deeply we have fallen asleep and that there is no room for complacency in my growth. Your journey and your desires may not be the same as mine and that's ok. You are not running out of time no matter what anyone tells you. Neither do you need to spend your time trying to save the planet and chant for peace. Those are all external approaches and as always the greatest gift that you can give to this game is to focus on your own realization and your own awakening to yourself…you represent the whole! But should you desire to experience the game from that perspective you are of course welcome to that experience. You are here to enjoy yourself in whatever way unfolds in your mind…all levels of emotions. You don't have to be anything for anyone!

This upcoming cycle will bring new health issues, as this programming is part of the cyclic theme unfolding. This has been in the making…an insert into the minds or the wiring of humans for the past few years. The healthcare bill is simply a code that will impact the entire planet, as all nations will review their healthcare policies. This involves all people; those practicing alternative health and those practicing conventional medicine. There will be battle between the two minds and those in the alternative health consciousness will not realize that they too are part of the game. There is fear of germs, viruses, N1H1 and so many more new health scares that will be in store for the human mind. Many people will be distracted and become obsessed with staying healthy; we will argue over raw food or vegetarian, fruitarian or pescaterian…oh this is going to be funny! We are already doing this so this will be turned up a notch. We are a gullible group but don't beat yourself up, this is all part of the dance. I have played it too and am recovering from it.

Learn to do whatever it is you do simply because you want to not based on an overabundance of fear otherwise you will create more of what you don't want.

Don't set yourself up with New Year's resolutions and then feel like a failure when you are not able to comply. The engineering of the human experience has been a masterful design and I do hope that you will join me at the upcoming lecture titled **Ascension of the Soul & Moving Beyond Destiny and Fate!** , January 30, 2010, Los Angeles. Remember that 2010 can be different. You can utilize the programming associated with this cycle and begin a transition beyond the "linear time" programs designed for the human experience. Point 0 is not the final point contrary to what is "believed". Let's discover more in this fascinating expedition we call "reality". Have a profound 2010! Much love to you all, my fellow explorer!

21

The Science of What Matters

Throughout the course of our lives we have heard the phrase "it doesn't matter," or "it matters." Little attention is given to the deeper connotation of these words. The idea that something "matters" or doesn't "matter" is a direct reference to the need for it to take shape or form. If it *matters,* this would imply that it is necessary for it to take on form, to materialize, whether physically or emotionally. We are giving permission for it to move out of waveform into particle form. If it does not *matter* then there is no need for it to take shape or form; no need for it to move out of its waveform.

Our lives are based on the things that matter to us, but upon close examination we might be quite surprised to realize where emphasis has been placed. Exactly where have we placed our emphasis? What things seem to matter? That which matters exist as the substance of our material experience, for when it does not matter then it does not exist for us. However, it might matter to someone else, and therefore exists in an allotted time and space designated to accommodate that which *matters,* or will materialize. Ultimately our reality is constructed of only the things that matter. Therefore all that seems to exist in the invisible holds a space of invisibility from our sight, because such things have no relevance to us at the moment; they do not matter in our current paradigm. When it matters, then components of the invisible will materialize.

It is amazing to think that we have used these words an incalculable number of times to create reality. We *pay attention* to the things that matter. Here we have it once again: a set of words heard throughout our lives, from our parents, school, work and those in authority. So what currency are we using to *pay* attention? We are using our energy to bring things into focus. Our applied *attention* is really a projection of energy, or more specifically, a navigation of emotions, which are electrochemical impulses. So, we make payment with the thought or emotion behind the energy output. Since we know that it is the science of observation — the focus of the observer — that creates reality, then we can more clearly see how we create those things that we give focus to; those things that we *pay attention* to.

Collective reality is a result of a group effort of determining what matters, and in so doing what we see before us as a common experience are those things that we have each agreed matter. This formula can be seen in full effect in an entire culture or race of people. The media has assisted in planting seeds in our minds about what does or does not matter, and so we materialize those things through the power of suggestion. The same holds true with projections through movies, spiritual leaders, education, government and the corporate structure. We are constantly being reminded of what should be important, or what is expected to be important to us. The subtlety of the suggestions is clever. We are prompted to *pay attention* to the impending doom of the environment or of the potential doom of 2012. What matters, paper or plastic or an environmental bag? Which do you choose? Do you choose out of fear, or do you choose based on your own personal preference? This simple process of consumers switching from plastic to carrying their own environmentally-friendly bags shows the easy manipulation of the human mind based on information cataloged and fed to consumers, who will more than likely not do their own research into what they are being told. Much of this new environmental programming is simply more of the same old manipulation by those who determine what should matter. The energy of the masses is always needed to construct the vision of what collective reality should look like. They need you to *pay attention*. The Poverty program is quite prominent in people of color throughout the planet, and is reinforced by the manner in which the rest of society is encouraged to *pay attention* to this matter. Both sides lend energy to an acceptance of a people in what seems to be irreversible poverty. The minds of an entire race of people hold this *matter* in focus as an accepted fate. Those who understand this science do all that is necessary to hold this program in place, with the support of an unsuspecting society.

why?

Since we are experiencing reality on the material plane, then everything here matters to us. We don't seem to deviate from the pattern of reality we hold in focus. There is no deviation from the base structure or model of reality.

DEFINITIONS FOR MATTER

> *Matter is a general term for the substance of which all physical objects are made.*[1][2] *Typically, matter includes atoms and other particles which have mass. A common way of defining matter is as anything that has mass and occupies volume.*
> *http://en.wikipedia.org/wiki/Matter*

1. *Something that occupies space and can be perceived by one or more senses; a physical body, a physical substance, or the universe as a whole.*
2. *Physics. Something that has mass and exists as a solid, liquid, gas, or plasma.*

http://www.answers.com/topic/matter Britannica

The Patriarch Hui-neng "Our Essence of Mind is intrinsically pure. All things are only its manifestations, and good deeds and evil deeds are only the result of good thoughts and evil thoughts respectively. Imagination, thought and will make deeds, and by our deeds we make ourselves. All that we are is the result of our thoughts; it is founded on our thoughts, made up of our thoughts."

Although matter is not the end–all of the creative process, it is, however, of extreme relevance in the process of arriving at the material level of reality. While the material world consists of mass, volume and weight equating to solidity, it is mind that forms the foundation upon which reality stands. It is consciousness that defines the level of mind shaping what will matter.

Perhaps it's time to re-evaluate those things you have placed importance on, those things you have paid much attention to, and those things you've deemed to matter. How much life-force have you expended on things that, perhaps with more clarity and insight, might not matter? Everything that matters must be supported by the energizer of that creation. We are the umbilical cord to our creations. Those things that seem to matter or take form also include our struggles and our belief systems. This kind of emotional engagement has weight and can become quite draining as we continue to support and focus our attention on them without resolution.

In this article it is important to briefly examine the three states of Matter and their behavior:

GAS
Assumes the shape and volume of its container
Particles can move past one another
Compressible
Lots of free space between particles
Flows easily

LIQUID
Assumes the shape of the part of the container which it occupies
Particles can move/slide past one another
Not easily compressible
Little free space between particles
Flows easily

SOLID
Retains a fixed volume and shape
Rigid - particles locked into place
Not easily compressible

Little free space between particles
Does not flow easily
Rigid - particles cannot move/slide past one another

Take note of the similarities and differences between all three but most importantly examine the behavior of the *solid* state: its fixed, rigid, not easily compressed and not much free space between particles. Now examine the nature of the human experience in the physical world and the fear of change and movement. Whatever we lock into, we stay there. It's a struggle to move from a familiar position or experience, and so it is with our addiction to the collective model of reality by which we operate. These vehicles are made up of solid matter, which reinforces our fear of expansion or change. We emulate the behavior of the particles. The irony of the "matter" is that the behavior of the wave and particle interchange is dependent on the consciousness of the observer of the experience.

This insight into the science of what matters caused me to examine and re-evaluate those things that might well be creating interference to changing aspects of my storyline. Your storyline is being held in place because it encompasses a great many things that matter to you. It's therefore challenging to change the habitual story because you are no longer aware of where your emphasis has been placed. Supporting your story and *paying attention* or focus to it has become an automatic process, so you no longer see that you are lost in these matters. A key realization now is that nothing is final and that becoming aware of this simple but impactful understanding can, in one afternoon, shed light on what will matter or perhaps will no longer matter to you. This can result in liberation and self-realization that you may not have felt for quite some time. It matters, it matters not!

22

A Bad Economy...A Mind Program or an Opportunity to Expand

One can hardly escape the overdose of news reminding us of just how "bad" the economy is. The gas prices were lowered as our minds were moved into the new alternate theme or chant of just how "bad" the economy is. Human beings adjust quite easily from one program to the next. Just a short while ago the high gas prices brought unity, common ground and common conversation to people from all walks of life. If we had nothing else in common we could participate in a conversation regarding the severity of the gas prices and just that quickly the human mind shifted effortlessly into the new theme...the new upload. We have transferred that same commitment to discussing the "bad economy".

As humans we enjoy chit chatting about such circumstances despite our argument of dread for such experiences...never the less we enjoy discussing just how "bad" things are. The feeling of helplessness always sets the stage or validates our need for a savior. This allows us to blame our dependency and false sense of security held for most of our lives; we can now blame its collapse on someone else. There are many arguments around these statements made, some may say yes but what about these poor people who need these jobs in order to put food on the table, in order to feed their families. The complexity of our individual journey plays a great role in the story by which we live life as individuals. The disabling effect of monitory limitation is only one small piece of the puzzle therefore we can feel compassion for those experiencing such circumstance. Very few emerge from such dark conditions and rise to wealth. We must once again recognize that money is a catalyst and sets the stage for the unfolding of a great many experiences in each of our lives.

We bring a great many debts, ancestral imprints and acquired imprints into the outline or map of life. This of course determines the families we will be born to as this is most often the starting point from which our lives take root regardless of the direction one may be drawn to.

Money provides freedom on many levels; however the question is what "levels" of freedom can you as an individual encounter which is within the realm of non-interference of those experiences essential to ones journey in this timeline. Remember that we are evolving our lives beyond the material plane…at least that's the objective as we move through the human experience (spiritual beings having a human experience.) For quite some time now we have surrendered ourselves powerless to the provisions of money as we accept the idea that without money we cannot bring our dreams to life. Instead we dream about having lots of money in order to purchase the dream of freedom. If indeed the overall objective of human life is spiritual evolution then it would stand to reason that there are a great many transitions in the life of an individual from one lifetime to the next allowing each soul to gradually emerge from his/her state of limitation and spiritual memory loss. There are a great many people with unbelievable monitory wealth yet remain quite distant from a more heightened state of magic in being more than mere flesh and blood. All of their physical needs are completely taken care of but yet there is tremendous limitation in other aspects…but yet this is the course of their journey. It's all playing out exactly as it should. So the question is what is the distance that you have chosen to go in this life, for it is evident that all of your circumstances are tied into numerous stages of our individual spiritual evolution.

Although we can change our circumstances at any time by changing our perception; many experience great challenges in doing so because of the interference being run by the inner programs. We are faced with literal interference or interception from these static programs; some carried over from one lifetime to the next others are acquired programs or ancestral imprints embedded in ones genetics. So the reconstruction of our perception in regards to wealth is heavily tied into a great many concepts and subconscious programs. Now it is possible to shift ones perception to acquire monitory wealth? This of course does not mean that one has been freed from the other levels of limitations to which one may be a spiritual slave. The freedom that money would present, could present and does present quite often propels one into a zone of having it all as one is completely unlimited in what one can now own and accomplish. For some the experience eventually wears off and the inner hunger returns, one which money cannot purchase or cure; although it can provide the freedom to go in search of oneself without the burden of the provision of daily sustenance. Most wealthy people spend time finding ways to create more wealth and in the meantime, they age, they become diseased and they also die. In some cases money temporarily extends their life and slows down the ageing process but it's still a temporary process. It is still however the experience they choose and they too have experienced such levels of limitation to the fullest just like the rest of us although our limitations may have been the extreme of absolute poverty.

So the ideal experience of absolute wealth begins with spiritual wealth as one has then tapped into an infinite flow of the substance from which all springs forth. All things physical and nonphysical is supported by energy in one form or another. It is then important to examine the hype being offered by so many in terms of acquiring monitory wealth. We must examine all that is attached to the haves and the have not's; the wealthy and the poverty stricken, we must recognize that although it's simply a matter of perception, the perception of each individual is tied into something much deeper than mere disbelief in his/her own abilities. The law of cause and effect is strongly tied into our perceptions and our spiritual status, for every action there is a reaction. More than likely you as an individual are unraveling from actions which may have resulted in reactions which now navigate your life as balance is sought. Tremendous difficulty come into play when we continue to repeat those same actions which continue to create streams of debt as we then pay dearly...sometimes with our life. We can continue to fool ourselves about who we are or what we have been although a great many things are tied into our unconscious. For some there is a stirring that takes place propelling them to take the plunge into the inner sanctuary. It is that journey that begins the purification process. It is that journey that begins to establish an unlimited sense of freedom.

I can and have examined times in my life where my cash flow was null and void, circumstances which drove me into deeper levels of survival which then validated my acts of desperation. Although I was aware that such acts were temporary solutions it was all that I could see as a way out, I was unaware of the backlash and perhaps did not care to know that there would be a backlash from these actions. However these experiences would later serve as a canyon in rocketing me into surrendering as I eventually crashed and burned from operating from a desperate space. What I discovered was that my desperate acts only perpetuated more of the very thing that I was running from which was the economic drought in my life. My desperate quest for money kept my mind programmed for scarcity and an ongoing fear of not having. I had to break the cycle. I had to go cold turkey; I had to walk the plank knowing that I would not fall despite being unable to see the invisible net below me. I realized that I had to go the process without accumulating more debt (spiritual debt let alone my debt to others). All the debts were tied in together. Deep down I knew that I was being deceived by my perception of money I recognized that my mind was programmed like most people to operate only on what could be seen by the physical eyes. I like everyone else was taught that without money I was immobilized, that I could do nothing, that I could make nothing happen unless I could see the cash before me. Once I surrendered to myself as source I had to commit to trusting the process, I had to decide that since I knew that my desire and my needs could be met regardless of the illusion of lack before me I surrendered to a knowing that my light bill would be taken care of somehow, my water would be taken care of, my rent would be taken care of; Notice that I said *"taken care of"*, I did not limit the resolution to "cash". I had made up my mind to stay the course even if everything was pulled from underneath me. I had to…it was the only way that I was going to break this cycle of desperation. I knew that if I stepped back into my old patterns of desperation to solve any of these problems I would jumpstart the process all over again and I would be right back where I started from. I just had to do it! I had to allow the old programs by which I had been operating to be revised into forming a new model of reality, my reality, my perception.

My severe financial circumstances thrust me into a new angle of desperation. I was now desperate to see behind the wall of the physical world. I wanted to operate as a conscious conduit. I wanted to be in full alignment with the unlimited flow streaming from the realm of the invisible. Again I will go back to the question I posed earlier; what is the distance that you chose to go in this lifetime? For it is the length of that distance that will determine your experiences, if all that you want is to be monetarily wealthy in this lifetime and you have achieved that then all of these actions in your life from the day you came out of your mother's womb has ensured this outcome. Some may want to be wealthy in this lifetime yet try as they might it never happens…to you I would say be brave and examine the entire course of your life up until this moment, examine your relationships with all people and the experiences of those relationships, search for themes in your life by that I mean patterns of experiences which seem to present themselves over and over again although the faces and the situations may appear to be different. Perhaps this pattern/s maybe the stumbling block to your limitations, perhaps once you acknowledge the pattern/s and seek to resolve these patterns which are more than likely tied into your personality, you may then be able to remove them from being the filter or the platform on which your life has been built.

23

Operating Outside of the System's Protocol

During the past several weeks I have stepped into levels of understanding about the nature of creation, taking me even further outside the normal protocols of reality as experienced by collective consciousness. Such interception has a profound effect on every action in one's life even the most mundane of everyday actions. This is all relative of course as we all experience a shift in our reality as we are impacted by the minutest change. This becomes interesting as others will express to you that they understand what you mean or what you are experiencing yet you know that they don't. How can that be determined? For myself I determine the possibility that such a person truly understand my current position simply by an observation of their action, by their language, their belief system and their thought process. This does not mean however that their experience is disqualified or of less value than mine but it simply means that we are on two different wavelength of experience.

The content of upcoming lectures clearly expresses the direction of information unfolding within me at this time. Many continue to wonder how it is that I am able to access this information and my response is generally the same, "I do not have a lid on what the potentials are, I am not afraid to see what it is that we are or how we were designed". Now I do know that a number of people will be quick to say that they too do not have a lid on creation nor are they afraid to discover what it is that we are but their actions and their responses tell me otherwise. While I may not be from this neck of the woods in terms of Earth as we know it to be, I am here just like you and I know what my objectives are at this time in the game and that would be to continue to spread out into forever but from an ever expanding consciousness instead of a sleeper. The issue is that humans are afraid of being disqualified from being what they think they are, but what I am showing is that yes consciousness is the ultimate force in charge but these bodies and this experience is a construct ran by cycles which operate like computer programs. Our universe is a system of program streams written to provide a specific kind of outcome or experience. However this can all be overridden if we will allow ourselves to truly examine the truth of what we currently are and what we continue to be unless we awaken. The engineering of this reality construct and programs are relentless and are cleverly written so no matter how you attempt to transcend them they loop you into yet another simulation.

Now let me engage you further in the new realizations that have come about in my consciousness. Humans fear the thought of being insignificant or not special so concepts outside of our comfort zone of indoctrinations are quickly tossed aside for more comforting concepts. However it is the discovery of the kinds of information that we shy away from that actually hold the key. Throughout all historical texts pertaining to spirituality or human existence it is noted that very few will find the door at any one time in any given cycle of evolution. This conclusion becomes more evident each day as people scramble to hold on the old beliefs inserted into their minds and within the overall human program by more aware forces both on the planet and outside of our planet's terrain. It is necessary to recognize that all that we create in the name of technology is mirrored from the engineering of our own construct as physical beings. We are also mirroring the design formula of the universal system and all-inclusive systems known as planets; galaxies, solar systems etc. The entire procession operates based on cycles to which we are tied. These cycles are on a timer which creates a domino effect of cycles from beyond zero point right through to this third dimension. However these cycles are program streams no different than a computer program. We naturally want immediately imagine that this spiral of cycles descending from beyond zero point is the totality of all creation; it is not! It is simply a separate program stream directly related to a specified reality with its own unique protocols. That program stream is coded based on a "what if" blueprint for a human being! Not every experience in core consciousness involves the model of a human being or the human experience. Therefore humans are generated from a specific set of programs. Who generates these programs? Well this is where system lords/engineers come into play or system architects. These are simply aspects of core consciousness operating at various levels of the descending program stream. They operate based on the original imagination of the "what if" consciousness; the processing of potentials and possibilities endlessly exploring itself. Remember that all that exist are concepts. The idea of a ruling God is derived from these engineers/architects. They however maintain their position while incorporating aspects of their consciousness into this experience we call the third dimension. These are the life forms on the planet we call human beings; the you and the me along with all forms of life on the planet including the planet itself!

In steps our obsession with Ascended Masters and guides. They are all programs coded into the general experience of the planet. Not only are they a program construct but they were incorporated during a certain cyclic shift in human evolution as watchers/ guardians and regulators of reality as perceived by humans. Once humans made their way onto the planet operating from a diminished mindset in these physical bodies, some thought it essential to position certain archetypes into the game experience. So we were wired/programmed with the savior/lord and master/god program, which we hold dearly to at this time. This is perhaps the most limiting program designed for a human being. Next came the death program to which humans are wired. Although these bodies are robotic and designed with a deeply rooted set of programs they can be overridden however the programming is so deeply rooted that one looks forward to an expiration at the end of a determined cycle. With the aid of much of these programmed inserts to which humans look for guidance, in the past 15-20 years humans have been more strongly encouraged to look forward to the afterlife. A sudden surge of near death experiences were wired into the experience no different than the countless themes that have come and gone in these cyclic processions. Humans are more confident than ever that they should go towards the light. What is the light? This is another space of existence that one's consciousness is ushered into. There was a surge of books and experiences by those having near death experiences and going towards the light, this allowed them to return and encourage others that it's ok…it feels really good…go ahead and "expire". Well once again in this shrewd game with all of its trickery and twists and turns humans do not exist long enough in their bodies to override a certain set of programs which have their own expiration dates if only we could hang on long enough to acquire enough memory/knowledge. It is why you must "expire" so soon for this disallows you to discover more of what you can be. I will not bombard this article with the science to support my conclusions but I hope to share that aspect in upcoming lectures.

There are some that will disqualify what I am presenting and that is ok…you see the system counts on the fact that the majority will disregard this truth but I am providing it none the less for those who will recognize what it is that I am sharing; those who will find a resonance. Again you may ask how do I know these things, I will tell you this much, I have not acquired this knowledge from channeling any external forces but rather from a place within me that maintains an aware existence in all potentials and in all pockets of that which exists and that which does not exist. I am technically no different than anyone. This is what I share with you and perhaps it is your time to move about in a more profound manner.

This kind of unfolding knowledge which I have touched on is not doubt shifting my life to OPERATING OUTSIDE OF THE SYSTEM'S PROTOCOL. This is challenging as things crumble around you yet you cannot reach for the same solutions for those solutions are only associated with who you were prior to this heightened level of understanding. So what do you do when your world seems to fall apart around you, well this is where you begin to reflect on the new knowledge and hold steadfast to knowing that you are becoming even more of a magician. You begin to recognize that you are entering a new field of thought and with that occurring a new reality must be created, new people, new concepts a new life. Is there fear? Yes because you are wondering into unchartered territory and it does not matter how many times you may have experienced a shift they are all different and where you end up will hopefully be different than the old patterns you left behind. Although you will continue to observe the outer world the emotional impact of these disasters and survival displays and the general motion of the world is seen, felt and experienced differently. You do not pray for peace and you do not pray for unity but instead you see a reality/people that/who do not need to be saved but rather to be given compassion if that is felt and honor them for their bravery in being part of such an experience. We all graduate from many levels of experiences but we simply do not all discover the door at the same time. This is simply the nature of the game. I know that there are many preaching about humanity moving collectively towards a brighter day...well again this is all based on perception so there will be collective shifts into various constructs and concepts of existence and none will be the wiser as to their advancements or setbacks. Yes that's the nature of the game; wherever you lay your hat is truly your home so why would you question anything. What I have learned is that you keep moving...moving in unlimited awareness, no limiting belief systems, no ritualistic practices that keep you trapped for years without you adding dimension to those practices.

I do hope that I was able to bring a bit more clarity to the direction of information that I will be presenting as I gain even more insight into an even more profound level of awareness yet to come.

24

The Unseen Dynamics of Operating in a Group
"Its effects on you may surprise you"

In making our way through this life; in having a circle of friends, belonging to an organization/group, being close to family or even operating in ones work environment or overall environment; is of great significance in regulating the movement of our lives. Quite often the impact and the influence of such group dynamics are overlooked. The influences are subtle. One individual in a group can sway an entire group in such subtlety leading the entire group to a common conclusion yet leaving everyone believing that their decisions were based on their own organic thought uninfluenced by others.

The psychology of group mind function is known and has been studied by those who seek to control; after all it is how we as human beings have functioned in collectively holding this concept of reality in place. It is a common and familiar way of being for human minds. Not only were we programmed to operate in this manner but these were conscious agreements prior to this third dimensional life as we've come to know.

Understanding the impact of groups especially those we have bonded with can shed quite a bit of light on some of the circumstances we face in our daily lives or perhaps for lifetimes. Although we bond together for support and in our attempts to connect with others of like mind we must also realize the limitations imposed by long term positioning in such groups. We are most often brought together because of a commonality, some sort of common ground in thinking or beliefs but such commonalities can lead to stagnation as we become committed to remaining in these groups. Growth means movement and most often the dynamics of a group is based on growing together, but what if everyone is not growing at the same pace? Sometimes incorporating ideas or concepts outside of the original foundation of the group might not be accepted as everyone might not be able to see what you are seeing. For some they may simply suppress their growth and remain in the group/family /environment or they may develop the courage to move beyond the group. They may even fool themselves into a sense of contentment if there is enough hype to keep them coming back.

Be aware of this fact; health problems, financial problems, relationship problems, fears, and any other experiences taking place in any group format will and can run like electrical current throughout the group attacking or attaching to weaker aspects of different individuals in the group. Sometimes a number of individuals in the group begin to develop similar symptoms or health disorders or financial upset etc. In one way a "one mind" function has taken hold. I have seen the fears of one individual spread like wild fire through a group without anyone being the wiser. You might not always be influenced in this manner but you can also be caught in a stagnating hype which is quite common! Once a week meetings or so that will hype up the individual for a period of time "positive thinking" as they say, nothing deep just the same old same old being repeated in different ways. It's comfortable and convenient especially in having to function in the madness of day to day life. In society most of us can attest to people being a bit put off when you express that you are vegan, vegetarian, raw food practitioner, home schooling or whatever it may be, many people functioning outside of the realm of your practices become a bit put off because it throws them off of their own function under the umbrella of commonality. They become a bit perturbed and will at times attempt to convert their fears by translating those fears into implying that you are the one with issues as you are operating outside of the norm. It is amazing to watch. Religious members are conditioned to do just that; if you are not part of a common belief system you are an outcast. Many people do not want to be an outcast so the human mind matrix is setup to provide a number of options so that we are caught in one or another collective thought process. Again the game is trippy and unless we can take a look at ourselves we will continue to be caught in this cat and mouse game. The nature of the game says that 'you must belong to some format of collective thinking". Why is this necessary? Because group mind and commonality keeps you fractured! Through group mind and collective thinking you are generally "this thing" or "that thing", are you a vegan, eat raw food, eat only fruits, eat meat, eat only chicken and fish, eat only fish etc., when these combinations are in the same group you will find that people who are not vegans, or raw foodists etc. begin to feel a need to explain that they don't eat meat all the time or whatever the case maybe. The point is that we are triggered when we are not all doing the same thing and we have a tendency to look down on others when we believe that we are operating from for a much more evolved space. This kind of subtle thinking is itself fracturing. It disallows you the freedom to be unlimited in a great many ways although unrealized. It forces one to keep up the charade; you must keep the mask on as everyone is admiring your ability to be so "holy" in your commitment. We place tremendous pressure on ourselves and others.

We must realize that typically people in a group do not grow together at the same rate and therefore we must enter such experiences without the commitment of permanency to a group/family/work environment or overall environment etc. Otherwise we will become caught in limitations without realizing it. This is not to say that we cannot participate or be part of our family and groups. The outcome of the circumstances which I witnessed was already known but I needed to see it play out in order for it to no longer be a theory but a fact. When one is entangled in fear, although we all have some degree of fear; especially when the individual has lived with these hidden fears or the root of those fears all of his/her life they learn to camouflage these fears and to influence and manipulate others into operating in a manner which will incorporate the unsuspecting individual into the field of that persons fear(s). The unsuspecting individual is fed a series of information that gradually conjures up thoughts and beliefs necessary to participate in the world of the "fear initiator". The extent that the human mind will go through to protect the individual is amazing and brilliant, it's an amazing protective mechanism which we all have. Rather than being discovered as a "fear initiator" the individual finds a way to bring you into their world, how brilliant is that! Most people will not notice for quite some time. Everything that you attempt to do in your life can then be influenced by the intertwining of your energies with this individual or individuals. We must wake up and step forward as individuals willing to face the journey completely alone so that we do not become stagnated when we encounter group energy, we can dart in and out freely. Group energy can also be parasitic. Anyone belonging to any one organization for 10 years and 20 years should perhaps step back and review the entirety of one's journey through the course of those years. Now, I do realize that we are getting exactly what we need for however long we need it. All that I am relaying to you is that perhaps it's time to examine ones reason for still being there, what do you continue to come away with and perhaps examine the level of knowledge depth you are seeking. Some will say that they enjoy the fellowship, but exactly what does that mean to you. You might say that you want to help humanity but again the best way to help is to move forward, the best way to help is to let go of your crutches. Groups are fun and can be enjoyed and utilized in a manner of individual growth when the entirety of the group realizes and understands the nature of the group mind process. When individuals can recognize and admit to their fears they too can move on, when individuals in the group can trust their own thoughts without question or doubt then they will no longer be influenced by such individuals and in turn this will be of great assistance to such an individual as their will be no one in any group or any individual around them to enter their world of fear; their lifelong camouflage.

They are then forced to deal with those hindrances in their subconscious mind. They will no longer manipulate. It will free them to live without this silently scheming mechanism within.

Women pay attention to the hormones and cycles of other women with which you are bonded. As you know when women are together they influence each other's cycles. This holds true even if you are no longer menstruating. Bringing this understanding to the forefront of your mind will then require that you make a conscious choice to have your body operate in its own natural cycles and not based on others. Sometimes we simply pick up a fear of developing certain conditions being experienced by other women. Determine your own course; determine what you choose to experience with your own body despite family and supposed hereditary conditions. We can choose!! You've chosen this life so what's to stop you from creating it how you see fit, you are already doing so anyway.

It is the reason for today's educational institutions, religion, modern day government and the media, for the purpose of indoctrination, developing and sustaining group mind thinking. Children are being programmed to conform, look around at your neighborhoods with track homes and the concepts embedded of a middle class or lower middle class or the entire class system. There is a group mind concept running through many systems and although we might not all be living the exact same life, there is a collective understanding of what images, attitudes and material possessions determine ones status. There is a base level of collective thinking, root concepts from which all other concepts are measured and formed regardless of one's race, religion, profession etc.

I urge you to examine your own life, the transitions which occur in your life when certain individuals come and go from your space. Examine your change in mood or abundant flow when with or away from certain individuals or groups. You need not abandon these people; you will simply need to take conscious responsibility for the fluidity of your life force in all aspects of your life. These people may however fall away on their own, or you may choose to release them from the bonded nature by which they had existed in your world. Remember also that these individuals have provided you with an amazing opportunity to grow and to elevate your ability to maneuver the course of your life. See this as an opportunity to reach beyond what you could dare to dream as a possibility. So in the end a group experience can propel you once you awaken to its dynamics!

25

Breaking Character
You are an actor, stuck in character

As we face challenges in our private realities, on our private stage, we are caught in the performance, the drama and intrigue of the experience. The actor now believes that he or she is the character, the role being played. This is the dilemma that we all face. The characters we play are created from archetypes written into the script of this collective version of reality—we simply add uniqueness to these characters based on the stories we select to play out as our experience. Most of our characters are largely based on deficiencies. We are always in lack of something. This sets the stage for us to spend great effort seeking to fill a void. But in the process of filling that void a vast array of experiences are created to further support these deficiencies, leaving us most often with short-lived substitutions.

Breaking character is about removing oneself from the performance. This is the purpose of deep meditation, but you need not always be in deep meditation to achieve this experience, at least not in the standard manner of achieving deep meditation. To break character is to stop the theater of performances in your head. After all, your experiences are really happening in your head. You process everything in your head, you experience it all up there and your conclusions become the basis for the character you play, as you continue adding to it. An example of this would be questions that you may ask yourself about one person's feelings towards you. In your head you begin to gather evidence from previous interactions, then before you know it you have created a story supporting your conclusion that this person doesn't like you. What do you do with this assessment? You then create a series of conditions and signals to alert you to more of this coming your way. Suddenly this has developed into a handicap for you, limiting you from being more engaging, perhaps. As you become less engaging in your interaction with other or just in general your world has to adjust to accommodate your fears. This of course spills over into your entire reality. It becomes clear that you never break character. You never leave the stage because you are compelled to maintain the experience.

Experiencing our characters is so hypnotic that the thought of breaking character is unappealing. In breaking character we run the risk of change. We are typecast in our roles. It is challenging to switch characters. We have become the role. We believe that we are our poverty, our illnesses, our professions, our social status, our education, our spiritual identities, our success, our so-called failures, our human status; they are simply all characters traits. What are we if we are not that? We feel we must identify ourselves as something. To be undefined is a fearful position for most, for if you cannot be identified then do you really exist? What will people say?

When we break character by stepping away from the performance, we become centered. We are not this thing or that thing, and in this space of centeredness we can re-create the manner in which we would like to return to our play, our adventure. You can change the construct of the role you play. To see the manner in which you acquired this role is of great significance in removing yourself from the hamster-wheel of experiences. Consciously breaking character as needed allows you to simplify and resolve issues without the interference of the limitations of the character you have been playing. How was your character shaped? Is it from the traditions woven in your family's character tree? Are you shaped from your bloodline's character addictions? Have you inherited the character you now accept as who you are, is it final in your mind? Is your character woven from the shadows of the past? Have you convinced yourself that you are *"just this way"*? Have you confined yourself to a concept that you do not know how to change? What you think you are on the stage of life is only a character. To believe that this is who you are is simply part of the agreement in taking on your character. A great actor must make the part believable. This you have done so well that even you are convinced, and to convince you otherwise could be a dangerous feat to the one who attempts to do the convincing. However, there is no need to convince anyone that they are trapped in a character, for they must play out these roles. When we become tired of playing the same part repeatedly, only then are we ready to return on occasion to who we are beyond these roles. Our acknowledgment of this theatrical experience returns us to our creative space as writers of reality.

To recognize the dynamics involved in character building according to the script of this reality is to gain tremendous power over your material and mental manifestations. Ultimately this collective script has character evolution written into it, where one can experience mind over matter, a role quite opposite the limitations of mind interacting with matter, at least on a conscious level. The roles commonly played come equipped with boundaries allowing one to be blind to their existence. When we are ill we are in character. When I had an allergy attack I was in character, but when important projects arose I had to break character and put the sneezing on hold. However, once I was finished with the project, the sneezing returned! We have all experienced such moments. Falling in and out of love is part of the role we play. Disliking one another for reasons imagined or unimaginable is part of the role we play. We believe in all of our reasons for being what we are when we are performing. We believe in our financial dilemmas as we struggle, either with our riches or our deficits, while at opposite ends these characters are built of the same principle. One sees money as an end-all and another sees money as a means to soothe the many plaguing deficiencies experienced by the character, the role being played. Are both characters wealthy? Yes! They are wealthy in unseen possibilities and the power to shift their experiences. Our houses, our jobs, organizations we belong to, money, banking systems, businesses, cities, cultural expressions, relationships of all kinds—they are all props and background with a supporting cast for your performance. We have established amazing set designs according to the requirements of the character we are playing. Living in a shack or a mansion—it's still all a set or stage with props. The true essence of who you are does not experience lack or deficiencies of any kind, but rather dives into vehicles such as this body to experience variety and possibilities. The mortgage or rent that *your character* might struggle to pay does not really exist but exists only as an emotional experience tied to conditions within your character's role. We are experiencing the theater within the game. The game is about these grand performances. Each one of us is the star of our production. Your issues, imprints and programs are all tied to the character according to what the role calls for. Your character is your automated self!

"One of Bohm's most startling assertions is that the tangible reality of our everyday lives is really a kind of illusion, like a holographic image. Underlying it is a deeper order of existence, a vast and more primary level of reality that gives birth to all the objects and appearances of our physical world in much the same way that a piece of holographic film gives birth to a hologram. Bohm calls this deeper level of reality the implicate (which means enfolded or hidden) order, and he refers to our own level or existence as the explicate, or unfolded order. Put another way, electrons and all other particles are no more substantive or permanent than the form a geyser of water takes as it gushes out of a fountain. They are sustained by a constant influx from the implicate order, and when a particle appears to be destroyed, it is not lost. It has merely enfolded back into the deeper order from which it sprang.

GEOFF HASELHURST – "The central point here is that our mind represents our senses (due to our evolution based on survival) rather than providing a true picture of reality. However, reason tells us that matter is clearly interconnected (e.g. the earth orbits the sun) and that there must be knowledge flowing into matter to explain how we can see things around us. This is correct, and explained by the Spherical In-Waves which form the 'particle' effect of matter at their Wave-Center."

"Sonia, that all sounds good, but I am here, struggling! I understand all kinds of struggle and I also understand that we have the power to leave the stage, to break character for but a moment in order to change the game, the play. If you never break character you will never be able to change your circumstances. Certain actions ensure that you are always in character and that you never leave the stage. There are those who want to continuously talk about how severe their situation is. They don't really want solutions, and will generally shoot down any solutions presented to them. They see only obstacles to changing their situation—their attention span is short, and when attempting to break character they bring the character with them, and then complain that they can't focus.

How do you know that you have brought your character with you? When you notice that you keep thinking about all of your external conditions when you sit to meditate or to focus, when you can't stop thinking about your problems, when the dialog is relentless in your head—this is how you confirm that you have brought your character with you. STOP BRINGING YOUR CHARACTER WITH YOU!!! STOP SAYING WHAT YOU CAN'T DO!!! (This of course is only being said to those who wish to experience moments without the running script.) Even if you are at work you have the power to leave the stage, break character, go to the restroom for a minute or two. You enter that bathroom stall with the realization that *"I am only playing a character, this is not who I really am."* Say this with conviction, then you go silent, nothing needs to be said, and all that is left is a feeling of creating something new. You can do this anywhere, at any time. To convince yourself that you must sit in the lotus position in silence in order to break character and connect inwards is simply another part of the character you play. You can leave the stage at any time and in any crowd. It allows you to be the *observer*, without thought, without judgment, without the echoing of your character. From this space you can move into experiencing yourself as a conscious creator. Here you have the opportunity to observe a different character, a different role that you will play when engaging on stage.

For some the idea that we are playing a role is jolting. For them to accept such concepts may provide a sense of invalidation of their existence, perhaps bringing a sense of insignificance to those things that they had placed importance on. *"What will become of me?"* Well, you will continue to exist, but perhaps taking on a new character submerged in confusion about who you are, or perhaps you will find the courage to see a wealth of possibilities in what can be experienced. Perhaps you will no longer feel trapped by the life you have been living based your old character. These characters allow us a rich array of experiences.

So whatever it is that you are experiencing at this time, remind yourself that whatever challenge lies before you is but a result of the components of the role or roles you have played. Don't become lost in your head, for when you do you cannot see clearly, and you will only become more of the character you have been. Stop and take a break from the stage…it will all be there when you return, if you so choose. Break character and rewrite the script, not with old solutions from a worn-out role, but with fresh insight and a desire for change. Don't spend time energizing what you don't want, and if you don't want solutions, don't pretend that you do by complaining. When you are ready for change you will no longer complain, but you will simply begin to take character breaks; you will leave your role behind, along with the entire supporting cast. When you return to the stage you may find that all that had supported your production is slowly fading. Not to worry, no cause for alarm. If you have indeed reshaped your character, then so must everything around you be reshaped. Whatever you are dealing with, it's temporary, unless you choose to create an illusion of permanence. Breaking character is your ticket to change, for you are not your character, but simply an actor in your own production.

26

It's All About Your Private Reality/Universe
"There is Really Nothing Out there"

When we speak of reality as I have mentioned many times previously, we must place great focus on our individual reality. Yes it's clear that we are one, but as individuals we are fulfilling the collective agenda of experiencing reality from an angle of separateness. Our private reality is our own universe from which we experience the collective. This is important to recognize. Why is it of such significance? Because you are determining the manner in which you will experience what we view as *"out there"*; the collective.

In my book <u>The Holographic Canvas</u> there is a chapter titled *Characters in the Game*, this is also of great significance in understanding the model of reality you have created and continue to recreate. Every aspect of your life is significant, such as the following constructs:

- The town/city you live in
- The state you live in
- The neighborhood you live in
- The school you attend
- The people in your class
- The teacher in your classroom
- The company you work for
- The office you are in
- The people you work with
- The church you attend,
- The club you belong to
- Your driving route
- The person you bump into on the street,
- The car you drive,
- The color you choose

- Are you vegan?
- Are you vegetarian?
- Are you a meat eater?
- Are you a fruitarian?
- Are you a breatherian?
- The name brand you like
- The husband/wife you have
- The lover/girl/boyfriend you have
- Who your parents are
- The friends you have
- You children/ family members
- Your parents

The above list is just a miniscule aspect of those things which form your reality. With that said just how many of us are aware of the level of "energy" output required to hold our individual construct of reality in place. This is not something that we think about as our thought process is focused on generating additional fuel/power to sustain our private reality. The process by which we fuel our reality is comparative to the numerous power plants which are positioned in many places to provide power to specific areas and facilities. You are the power plant which runs your private reality. As you have read in my other articles and my book <u>The Holographic Canvas,</u> your consciousness is interwoven into all people, places, things, attitudes and beliefs. The characters in your life each require different degrees of fuel to keep them in your reality; some may require more of your life force than others according to your interaction with the character. If there is continuous contention, despise, drama, aggravation, frustration, heartache, etc. then these characters are an energy drain as they must continue to be there until you are satisfied with getting the fullest degree of experience that can be extracted. Each explosive interaction requires more fuel from you and so you are slowly being drained. These experiences can result in emotional conditioning, a programming of low self-esteem, low self-worth, distrust etc. Although these characters may disappear from your life if their purpose for having been in your reality have not been fulfilled then chances are that they will return again and again although the faces and the process of the experience may change. The question should then be asked, what is it that you needed to understand in your game, your reality.

To understand the degree of power output required to sustain your reality is perhaps the most significant realization that you can embrace as each moment is literally *spent* keeping the power going in your reality. The external world is only a result of the inner world being sustained by every individual who makes up the collective. With the current economic theme being played out, there is a tremendous amount of *power/fuel* (human energy as fuel) being emitted from so many individual losing homes, property, jobs, relationships etc. Again I am speaking of the energy/the life force from each individual used to hold on to what he or she owns. When we say that we have put our blood, sweat and tears into those things we hold precious this is absolutely true. Every fiber of your being is involved in the process of building and sustaining ones reality. We are emotionally interwoven into the core structure of our reality. Our emotional output is the fabric which holds the structure of our reality which then forms our identity. It is for this reason that when any portion of our reality is shaken by change it becomes a jarring experience to the very core of our being. We are somewhat shaken when the neighbor moves or there is a new cashier at the grocery store we have been going to for years. We struggle for readjustment when we make simple changes such as taking a different driving route than habitually done each day. For some being without an insurance plan or 401k is shattering especially if they have had it for years, some short circuit if they are unable to plan ahead for the most minute things.

Then there are those who will read this and say that they don't do any of those things but I can guarantee that should you decide to take an honest look at yourself you will realize all of the beliefs and conditioning that you are wired into. There is no way of holding those same old beliefs and conditioning in place without being hardwired into them and again remember that hardwiring requires a large "power output". It is your creation, it is your reality, your universe, your game and so it must be supported by the energy plant from which it was originally generated; YOU!. You have written one base script from which you have written all other scripts throughout the course of your private reality. These base scripts are generally based on imprints, deeply rooted programs, ancestral/bloodline baggage etc., and as we go along we incorporate social, cultural and environmental programming (Read Ancestral imprints). Your base script sets the stage for your acceptance of certain beliefs and experiences. Characters are then written into various scripts according to all of the above. We invite characters who will validate what we believe as well as those who will challenge those beliefs. We invite warring characters, controlling characters; we invite characters who will help us to test our boundaries. We invite characters who we can blame for everything in our lives just so we do not have to take responsibility, we invite characters who will treat us like door mats or those that we can treat like door mats in order to feel powerful, we invite characters who are easily manipulated, we invite characters who will keep us confused, we invite characters who will make us look like model citizens or spiritually powerful etc. The point is that we invite everyone into our world; no one enters without an invitation. It is the energy sent out through the field of consciousness that is read and picked up as a signal by the appropriate characters. You don't have to say a word…it's all about the energy field. Nothing is undercover as the frequency reading is available to all, especially those attuned to the bandwidth circulating.

If we do not begin to become aware of the manner in which we hold our creations in place, you will not be able to understand why you are having certain kinds of experiences that you as an individuals may be questioning. The manner in which you interact with collective reality or are impacted by collective reality will depend on what is needed in your private reality to complete whatever your script may call for. What is it that you still need to experience around certain emotions? What is your relationship history, romantic or otherwise, what have you been trying so desperately to achieve and at what cost, what is the foundation for your desire in wanting to achieve, are you still seeking security and what does security mean to you and by whose terms, is there any such thing as security, what are you afraid of, is money the root of all your struggles, is money what you strive for, are you striving to be rich, just how much stock do you place on money, in your mind is money a defining point, are you still looking for love, do you feel that love will bring you security, do you feel incomplete without a mate, are you defined by your material positions; characters will enter your life based on many of these reasons.

These are reasonings that take you outside of yourself, causing you to spend much time in your head...you run around in our head. Much of your life is played out in your head as you conjure up things about the past and the future, endless speculations about people and circumstances that only perpetuate more of the same old script. This simply brings in characters to play out your speculations and fears, which sets your mind at ease because you can now say that you were right all along when characters enter and wreak havoc in your reality or play out your speculation. This allows you to say things like "People always take advantage of me", "I try to help but I always get burned" "I am always unlucky in love" "I don't trust anybody" "that's why I always lock my doors" "it's a good thing I had insurance" "people are losing their jobs right now, you better do everything to hold on to yours" and on and on. Again ideas, concepts right down to the material world is held together by the power which surges from you. Remember that I am using the concept of "power" from the perspective of the juice/energy/fuel derived from you as a "power plant" to hold the very things in place which have become the illusion of your imprisonment to them. As always be reminded that it has all been a necessary process, you have been fulfilling all potentials in the human experience. No regrets on any of it! Just own it as the illusion that it is…it's a game.

The power being expelled by you as you hold your constructed reality in your consciousness has diverse extremes of where much of your power, your focus goes to…remember that those things that are the strongest part of your focus will require more of your energy, more power, more "charge" to hold it in place. So let's examine a few more "power drains" sucking power from most of our private realities and how we have bought into them:

THE CREDIT BUREAU

Many people are imprisoned to the credit bureau and the credit rating system. You buy into not being able to do a great many things unless your credit score is at a level defined by the rules of the game.

There are three categories of individuals with three different ways of handling this credit rating concept (1) some will make things up on the application as need be (2) others will work at maintaining an upstanding credit score (3) those who will settle for the level of limitation based on low credit scores as defined by the system (4) then there are those who have realized that they can have anything they want despite their credit score…and it can be done without survival tactics. Those in the category of 1-3 are playing the survival game…yet there is no right or wrong these methods however operate on limitations. You are confined to your "autopilot self" figuring out your "survival" and playing safe and hustling all at the same time.

THE BANKING SYSTEM

This is a major energy drain for many people. I am quite familiar. All that you see are numbers...you experience the energy of it according to the preset conditioning, the energy value, the quantative values allotted to the dollar. So it's only the energy of the implied monitory value that exists in the banking system. You are programmed into an agreement of this limitation. It is often said that money is being printed out of thin air...well in all honesty that is the way that your reality should operate!! Your monetary needs should arrive out of thin air! Instead we are committed to believing the rules of limitations set within the game. Once again be reminded that you are a spiritual being having a human experience which requires the illusion of extreme limitation in the game in order to experience both ends of the spectrum. In interviewing Professor Oyibo, Mathematician, a scientist who explained that we should want for nothing. According to Professor Oyibo we should be able to create all that we need out of thin air as everything is made up of everything, hydrogen being the common denominator in all things.

MONEY

Much time is spent acquiring an accumulation of money or simply acquiring just enough to get by. Most of the power output goes to supporting the desire for an increase in monitory abundance. This of course requires full focus for almost 24 hours per day even while we sleep. The collective concept of money ensures the static view of realty the illusion to which our consciousness is tied. We are the power source which holds these quantative values of limitations by which money is held in our consciousness.

THE INSURANCE SYSTEM

The concept of insurance is symbolic of the illusion of security. Insurance is the symbol for security plain and simple. The Insurance game represents the "what if" and the feared outcome. When one is in fear of being caught without insurance for health, life, auto or any other form of insurance it simply means that the possibility exists within ones field of consciousness for an associated experience. I am certainly not implying that anyone should get rid of their insurance I am simply bringing to the surface the subtle programs interwoven into ones reality. We are not always aware of these programs because we are simply operating on the premise of "doing the right thing". What is the right thing and based on what, where is that thought process or belief system stemming from?

THE MORTGAGE SYSTEM

This is another power-full game. People work all their lives to own a mortgage and spend all of their life's energy paying for it. You are interwoven into your property. Your property is an extension of you just like everything else that you have possession of. Even when one loses his/her property they remain tied into the property because they were unable to release it. The system ensures that by keeping your name against the debt owed. You feel trapped because you now believe that this is a mark against your name blocking you from obtaining another piece of property or other things. What is also interesting is that the bank does not loan you any money as many people are now discovering. Anyone can type numbers on a piece of paper it's all smoke and mirrors. The bank adds to its illusionary monetary resources only when you begin to pay the monthly mortgage will those illusionary numbers begins going up in the banking institution. Here is a definition of the word *institution* as taken from Wikipedia:

Institutions are structures and mechanisms of social order and cooperation governing the behavior of a set of individuals. Institutions are identified with a social purpose and permanence, transcending individual human lives and intentions, and with the making and enforcing of rules governing cooperative human behavior. The term, institution, is commonly applied to customs and behavior patterns important to a society, as well as to particular formal organizations of government and public service. As structures and mechanisms of social order among humans, institutions are one of the principal objects of study in the social sciences, including sociology, political science and economics. Institutions are a central concern for law, the formal regime for political rule-making and enforcement. The creation and evolution of institutions is a primary topic for history.

Now apply the word _institution_ along with its definition to all organizations you interact with including your corporate institutions.

BUYING ON CREDIT

Again this is tied into the credit rating system. Another amazing tool in the game which provides immense experience in accumulating things and going into debt in owning those things; buy now pay later...you pay with your life force, you pay with stress as bill collectors are calling you, you become worried about the drop in credit rating, how will you find a job now that they are checking credit reports, what kind of person does this make you and the collector reminds you of all of these things. This entire process keeps you in the loop of survival..."how will I ever get out of this?"

COLLECTION AGENCIES

The collections agencies are just that they are agents you invited in to attach to you as a power source. They assist in your emotional drain, they taunt you, they exert fear and with that each moment of your anger whether you pay them or not, they receive energy from you; you are angry and upset, you curse them, you hang up on them all of these emotions puts you in a dance with them. They are fulfilling their purpose as energy vampires in the game especially from the angle of the monitory system. They continue to reaffirm the value of the monetary system as collectively agreed on. They keep you reminded of "the limitations" in your thought process of the value placed on money.

THE RETIREMENT SYSTEM *retiring from slavery*

If you could live your life through a flow of experiences without the security of repetition and prepackaged directions leading up to your death then you would not need to move into a thought process of retirement. There would be no retiring...retiring from the pre-coded definition of the system/matrix is all about one's life force winding down to the countdown of death. You spend your entire life's energy, a huge investment of power preparing to die! Think about that!

RELATIONSHIPS

All of the above require a relationship with many characters. While you may play out much of your reality in your head, in your mind, this carries over into determining your energy exchange in all degrees of relationships. The bottom line is that every change you make in your consciousness will shift the relationships you are in. It does not matter whether that relationship is with a lover, a friend, family or a physical possession. Everything around you changes to adjust to any upgrade you make in your consciousness. It is for this reason that knowledge is so amazingly power-full. There is usable POWER (electromagnetic) in knowledge that can and will remove more and more of the limitations by which we have been experiencing our lives. It's never about the people around you changing. It's about you evolving your hologram of reality in your consciousness.

You power up your reality every step of the way. You are completely involved in the entire process. There is no one to blame there is no need to blame anyone, including yourself. Choosing to evolve the holographic structure of your reality will mean naked surrender, for these individual realities are the illusions which form the overall reality. You are in a cosmic game! It's important to nail the concept that you are in a game; one with no winners or losers however strategies are required yet anything goes. You are at the center of the story line throughout the entire course of your ride. I have often expressed that it's not about escaping from the matrix but it's about understanding that you control the entire outcome of your reality; all the players are in position just the way you positioned them. The question is, are you ready to take it to the next level of whatever that may be in redeeming freedom at greater levels.

Surveillance of society continues to increase. There are cameras everywhere and now digital boxes entering the homes. This can be viewed as symbolic with you as an individual setting up surveillance in your private reality as you observe: what does each character represent in your world, how many main characters are there, who is going and coming from your reality, how limited is your reality, what are the themes playing in your world, what is your belief system based on, what kind of tools are you using to stimulate an infinite supply of abundance to your reality or is it all based on programming. As I have stated before it is about freeing one's self from the illusion of enslavement to the system. What you must do is to free yourself from the imprisonment of the limitations in ones consciousness. Now that you have read this article and perhaps have stirred a realization of you being the power plant for your own imprisonment, you must ask the question "what am I willing to give up or to lose". First it is important to again remember that it is all an illusion in the first place one which you strongly affixed to in your validation of your own existence and in evaluating your status or progress in life. Your material possessions have become your scale of evaluation for your life's journey on the planet. All that you have done has been a beautiful accomplishment whether you have been pushing a shopping cart and homeless on the street or whether you live in a mansion or a matchbox, whether you have been in a mental institution or a professor at Harvard or a thief. It's all powerful because in one way or another we have all been a little bit of all these characters in our minds where nobody can see the depth of our thought process or that which lies in the catacombs of the mind. It all requires tremendous POWER to involve ourselves in any level of experience.

The trick however is in learning to dream and to create without the attachment...yes and I will say it again, it's all about moving fluidly, it's not about losing power to our creations. When we lose our power to what we have created, not only do we lose power but we lose memory of who we are as spiritual beings having a human experience and this is where we becomes the prisoners of our own creations. We can consciously support the structure of our reality. When our power is locked into our creations then the fluidity of abundances is then no longer the center of power as we must now focus on survival and this of course has nothing to do with money. To be rich with a numerical worth is still a limitation as our ultimate goal should be to return to drinking from an unlimited supply, feeding all areas of our lives. Infinite abundance has no numerical value, it's not possible...so what is my net worth, it is unlimited! Scientists like Professor Oyibo and Qunatum physicists are discovering how and why it is possible to consciously alter ones reality. You don't need to wait for University trained scientists to tell you that it is possible as you are creating your reality in every moment. You simply need to recognize this for yourself by observing the foundation on which your life is built along with an examination of your choices and beliefs.

You are an amazing power plant and perhaps the time has come for you to create a new and different concept of your reality. Perhaps it's time to exceed the typical, predictable programs by which collective consciousness is run. Listen to signs of boredom and consider what it would be like to do the things that bring excitement to mind, or what it would be like to lay down your burden of struggles if indeed there is a possibility that you do have an unlimited source of power that you have perhaps minimally tapped into from time to time during extremely desperate moments. What if you did not need to wait for desperate moments to utilize the science of the limitless? Many of you have heard me say that the manner in which I have accessed my jump through the various stages of my growth is to say to myself that "no matter what, I will live!" That has always been the deal breaker for me! In the past in leaving corporate America my son asked me "mom if they paid you a million dollars to stay would you" and without hesitation I said "NO!" You must come to the place where you can honestly say that it's not about the money, when you can make decisions based on what you feel in your gut, in your heart center, then you are ready to take that leap. It can be challenging but it has allowed me to go deeper and deeper into a knowingness that continues to blow my mind!!

This is what I now share with you; the ability to dig deep and to own your right to know and to be limitlessly powerful! It is a magnificent goal which I continue to explore, what an adventure! Don't be afraid to own what you are feeling despite being unable to share these feelings with your partner or friends, remember that it is all about you. They are only a reflection of your field of consciousness.

27

The Art of Standing Still

So often as we make our way through this journey we encounter many illusions set before us as stumbling blocks. We face the challenges of seeing beyond these blocks or walking through them as if they were transparent. Most often we stop to emotionally engage with the circumstance, the individual or just the feeling itself. Our engagement becomes the very substance that brings life to the illusion. Yet everything before us screams for our attention. Our involvement then defines THE RULES OF ENGAGEMENT. How long will we engage, and what is the intensity of the drama that will unfold.

I am speaking of those things by which the matrix/system operates; two of the main catalysts being money and relationships. When faced with deficiencies around these two energy eaters we are drawn in by the pull of its current. We are sucked in and we begin moving in rotation of the vortex. Complete control is lost as we seek to grab on to whatever we can to stop what seems to be an involuntary ride. The momentum most often forces one to the point of critical mass and when this happens desperation sets in and we scramble for dear life. This kind of scrambling will more than likely create off shoots of additional vortexes creating a spiral of challenges.

Fear and desperation become the controllers of one's life showing you only those options which will ultimately only provide temporary relief while rebirthing an endless cycle of more of the same. Try as you might your ability to stand still becomes virtually impossible as one is overcome by a need to control things on a physical level. Now one might argue that you have meditated on the matter and released it. But did your meditation consist of controlling the process of the outcome, did your release consist of a predetermined process to the outcome. In our minds we face the challenge of relentlessly trying to figure out a plan...going back and forth...telling yourself "ok I am releasing it". Heading for the point of full surrender is the objective. What does full surrender entail? It entails the surrender of "come what may", especially when you have done everything in your physical powers. This is the point where you stand still! This is where you let it all go. You won't die from it but things may change drastically around you.

Why is it happening in this manner? Well perhaps some time ago you had desired your life to unfold with a particular set of results and now everything in your life is being rearranged to build up to that moment. What did you desire? Amazing isn't it. You will have forgotten many of these things that you have desired yet the people you meet, your change of location, job etc has been leading up to it. Perhaps your desire was for deep spiritual knowledge/awakening you could be in the midst of a drastic shift! I often times hear people say this "I am so ready to know, I am ready to move forward spiritually", but they are never prepared for the process by which this will unfold. This can be like a drowning man struggling for air; one begins to struggle against the tide of change and panic sets in. "How can I regain control" that's the question posed by the autopilot self. "I am going down and fast", but you really aren't it's quite the opposite. You are actually rescuing yourself. We seek to hang on to the familiar despite the discomforts previously presented by the familiar.

What happens when your survival skills and instinct nudges you to force your way into choices already recognized as temporary, what can you do, and what will you do? It's like having a board meeting in your head and fighting against a corporate takeover. You are literally engaged in negotiations with yourself all in your head. Oh the game!! It's scary, adventurous, maddening and exciting all at the same time. What an adrenalin rush! Talk about getting your money's worth on this virtual/holographic tour. Oh yeah, you're having fun. It's like you are on a scavenger hunt. It's damn tiring and at times you just want to get the hell off the tour and ask for your money back! What was I thinking when I signed up for this big, little illusion…just what was I thinking! Yup that's what you are saying not necessarily in those words but that's pretty accurate. You do have a few people that do get off the ride one way or another…they come down with mental illness (escapism), suicide, denial, just an assortment of remedies. Well for me none of those are options that fall in line with my ultimate objective of finding my way out from under. Remember the scene in the matrix with Cypher, where he says put me back in! I understand completely why he wanted to be put back into the matrix, and it is the same reason why most people lock into their packaged beliefs and packaged lives. To step outside of the box requires taking responsibility for one's self and that can be overwhelming. The thought of letting go of secure jobs, relationships, relatives, friends and spiritual beliefs can be like a tornado ripping through one's mind. Here is an interesting de-ciphering of the name Cypher from the Matrix: Taken from Wikipedia Encyclopedia:

> **Cypher** - *Cypher's name may be a reference to ciphering, or encryption, which is commonly done to prevent computer documents and programs from being hacked. Cypher himself is very difficult to understand and his selfishness and treachery is hidden under a facade. The name is also a nod to the hacker subculture, which greatly influenced the first film. Cypher may also be related to Lucifer (Lu-Cypher), the Angelic name of Satan, referring to his actions in rebelling against Morpheus*

Although not noted here my explanation of the name Morpheus is a derivative of the word morph- definition: to be transformed or to transform. Morpheus is also the Greek God of Dreams; dreaming is transformational, shifting from one reality, one world to the next. This dream world is all consuming, appearing as the only reality and option. It is the bombardment of relentless emotional engagement with those things which shake our egos, those things which go thump in the night, the fear and programs ingrained in the patterns form which we each create our reality. Patterns stemming from childhood along with already embedded ancestral patterns woven into our consciousness. What would it feel like to just chuck it all…all of the situations that we work so fervently at protecting? Most of these conditions are generally ideals acquired from social expectations and acceptability's. What if you are struggling just to eat, feed your kids, and keep a roof over your head? What we call the basic necessities of life. Well from my own experience that's when I got most serious about evoking my will and my right as a creator; as creation itself. Although my understanding had not matured to the level it is at this time something in me knew that I could create and that it was my right to be provided for.

While I was undergoing such experiences as a single mother of two boys caught in deeply turbulent times it was my moment to grow, my moment to show myself who and what I was made of. No it did not all happen smoothly or like a fairytale so in the mean time I had to find ways to meet those needs. In came desperation…my judgment was not always clear but it was what I understood until I could nail more and more of who I am. My children traveled this dusty, rocky road with me and so we must understand that our children are completely on the journey with us. These are souls who decided to take that journey with you and perhaps knock it out the way so that they will not need to explore that road later on in their life. I can tell you that my children now 28 and 25 are vocally thankful for the process. They have an unbelievable understanding of the journey on all levels both physically and spiritually and it marvels me. So allow and honor your children as souls engaging in the journey with you. Co-partnering with you and following your lead.

Now in terms of those moments when you have run out of solutions…STOP…this is where you stand still…this is it right here…the defining moment, make or break, sink or swim. These moments may feel like death, yes it is the dying of the old making way for something new. It sometimes takes a couple of days of going back and forth before you are forced to let go, let it all fall and just know that it's not that you have given up but you are simply stepping aside to allow the greater part of yourself to see what you don't and take you through the process. Always remember that the greater part of you has your best interest at heart. These are truly defining moments. Once you let go then follow what you feel...do you feel like taking a long walk, or driving to nowhere special for a short while, do you feel like getting some ice cream, a drink, or perhaps a movie or doing nothing...maybe some music! I have driven up to the mountains or put music on and just danced in my car or in the house...the other day I turned up the music to "Piece of my Love" by Guy/Teddy Riley...yes I listen to whatever moves me at the moment, might be Tupac or Wild Cherry, "Play that Funky music " or Earth Wind and Fire, David Bowie...hey let it all go...that's how you shake it!! You don't need to qualify what you are listening to; it doesn't have to be serene music. This is how we destabilize those particles because you will have stopped observing them!! They have no choice but to shift, remember that you are the one observing your reality, your hologram into existence.

I am all about keeping it simple. Freedom comes from taking the pressure off of yourself, yes you are an aware traveler but who says that you have to do it by any one's rules. You only have yourself to answer to. You are your own judge and jury and with that said you have a choice as to whether you will sell yourself into someone else's beliefs. There are indeed forces which exist according to the terms you have established for yourself. You must take conscious ownership of yourself otherwise to say nothing leads to presumption and you become the property of illusionary forces. Stand still so that you can see clearly. The mind will then quiet down allowing you to slow down on creating scenarios that will become more of your demise. Remember that each moment is giving birth to the next moment and in those moments choices are being born. These choices are your chariot to your tomorrow.

This is only a glimpse into *"the art of standing still"*. There are other methods that may appeal to you; I go with what resonates with me. So although the challenges are staring you in the face stare back at them by standing still. I promise you will find resolve in the silence. My approach to consciousness/spirituality might be slightly different but it's a lot more fun than all the stuffiness and restrictions! Right now I am going to let it all go and kick up my heals to "Piece of my love"...mmm what will my tomorrow look like ...not sure yet but damn the music sounds good!!

28

The Illusion of Value and Self Worth

You are seeking value and self-worth from your relationships and you don't even know it. Value is an amazing phenomenon because like money value is a measurement of energy; emotional output. Little do we understand why we continue to encounter the tug-a-war experienced in our relationships. We want to feel as if we are valued and worthy of being part of any interactive experience. To desire to be valued is another limitation just as the limitations we have placed on money. Value like money is measured on a spectrum of being a little or a lot. The more we seek to experience a calculated value of our worth to another, it becomes more tiresome and challenging. It causes one to be in constant e-valuation (energy value) of the response being received from those around you especially one's mate. One party invests much time (the investment of time = energy output) doing everything to feel value or worth and the other struggles in opposition…most often not intentionally. We have all been on both sides of the spectrum. The effect is much like two magnets repelling each other. Neither party wants to surrender. Control is about value and worth! **ITS EMOTIONAL MONEY!**

This is the ultimate prize derived from competition; football, basketball, chess, grades, social status, monitory status, life etc.! The ultimate prize is value. We want everyone to acknowledge our worth, that's why we want to be a "good person" (whatever that is), we want to be upstanding citizens, we want to be well liked etc. The quest for value digs deep into our emotions and it's used to keep us at odds with each other, in school, in our corporate jobs, in our religious organizations. The hunger for value taps into our soul and we look down on others when they do not appear to possess the well-defined rules of "value". Again "value" is emotional money! So what are you saying Sonia? What I am saying is that if you could but for a moment step back and examine where you are, examine your role in any and all relationships with people are there some common threads that keep appearing. Do you find yourself in jobs where you just keep getting passed over or being continuously reprimanded, disliked, feeling inadequate or do you find yourself trying really hard and hoping to hear the words "good job" Notice the feeling that floods over you when you do hear "good job" and notice the feeling that chokes you when those words never seem to come. Not only do you want to be paid in dollars and cents you want emotional dollars as well! As I have written in the article <u>It's all about your Private Reality/Universe</u> I indicated that any quantative value given to money is still a limitation, well the same goes for any measurable value you may try to limit yourself to.

Our minds are clouded by the illusion of the game. This particular level of the game is based on all of the rules for this level of the game called "A LIMITED LIFE". To move beyond this level of the game you must remove the concept of measuring your worth! Your monetary condition is tied into your sought after "value". You are technically measuring the net worth of your life force! Again everything that you do is tied into this concept and you spend your entire life proving your worth. Some give in to the pressure of proving their worth and step off the ride; literally, others die from the stress, some simply find another reality in their minds to operate and those are the people we call crazy. The rest of us intellectualize our lives so that it does not appear as if we are seeking value and worth. We are amazing masters and game players! We are so amazing at disillusioning ourselves and with that same tenacity you've created this matrix, this illusion within which you find yourself feeling trapped and imprisoned. That's how good you are. You made the illusion so believable that you are having a hell of a time unconvincing yourself that it's not real, "but it has to be... how else am I going to find value and self-worth , but oh wait that's right I exist in an endless stream of consciousness, I am creation!"

The matrix now faces wars and the destruction of life, again all based on securing control, power over religious, political, racial and spiritual dominance. Who will own the rights to the real estate of the human mind, body and consciousness? Are you in the infinite flow or are you in pursuit of seeking value? Whatever your location on the planet, it is significant to your own personal evolution as each area provides a specific vibration of minds in resonance with your needs as a spiritual being having a human experience. Souls in lands of absolute poverty and war lay under a blanket of the contracts of that land. Each land is its own matrix with its own mission, its own rules of engagement for the experiences which will be presented or experienced in that land. There might be difficulty in understanding this concept but the facts speak for themselves. This is akin to the concept of culture as I have written about as well. Each country, each environment has its own culture by which a people will resonate collectively. There are things that are understood within other cultures which you may not so readily agree with. These are the collective tones by which they operate much of which is unspoken. These codes of culture are infused with value therefore there is pride in upholding these cultural codes. When one steps outside of these cultural codes one loses value, ones worth is lost among a people and it is with ease that cultures with ridged codes can without thought stone an adulteress to death or exile one of their own. Value must be protected at all cost. Religious beliefs have value to them and in that same manner they will annihilate millions of people to secure value; the measurable worth of the collective. The value of the individual does not matter in such cases as value is received from the collective.

We find that same premise in what we would call our modernized lives. Instead we fulfill the collective value by attempting to convert others to our religion or to force ones mate into some sort of value scale or by judging others whose life might not seem to fulfill the guidelines of the status quo. Oh yes the concept of value and self-worth goes much deeper than you may have thought, take a careful evaluation of your life right now, the challenges you may be facing right now in your romantic relationship as well as with those around you. Feeling as if you are being taken for granted is a big sign that you are in "value crisis" mode. You don't have enough emotional dollars coming in! Stop being taken for granted then, just stop; no one is making you do that. You have set this experience up, this illusion hoping that perhaps you would eventually get it and then awaken from this deception and retrieve your power. If you can manage to see this for yourself you will be amazed that when you snap out of this you will retrieve your power from every draining situation in your life right now!...why is that? Because I can guarantee you that pretty much all of your decisions and choices are running off of the same value scale, and they are all draining your power! Once you are able to do this things will change in your relationships as you will no longer be feeding these power draining conditions any more. You will no longer need validation and worth. You will no longer need to be defined by anyone. You now see your true self as an unlimited being that is infinitely abundant. As they say change your thinking and you change your life well you can't change your thinking until you get it! To simply memorize affirmation after affirmation is like dealing with hooked on phonics or singing the alphabet; it's just memorized information. It is important to understand concepts and ideas by which you have built your reality in order to create something new.

Many of you are having relationship challenges. I have said many times, do not worry about whether your mate understands this information or not, simply focus on you. Believe it or not your mate is serving a purpose far greater than you might be able to see at this time but you are unable to see what this amazing teacher is presenting to you, why, because you are busy seeing all of the things you don't like about your mate. You are distracted by that, the question then should be, why are you with him/her or they. When you are able to stop long enough to examine your position and set your ego aside for a moment you will see something beautiful and as

I said once you are able to wade through the dislikes you will understand why you are in your relationship and it will set you both free. (I am not saying that the s---t won't hit the fan when this realization surfaces) The relationship/s will then move to the next level one way or another. In the mean time you are caught in the emotional currency game just like the rest of the planet... all playing for emotional dollars! You are reading this article for a reason, stop and recognize that reason...now what are you going to do about it! We are no doubt trapped in our own minds and only you hold the key.

29

When Nothing Seems to be Working

There are those moments that many of us face when everything seems to freeze and nothing seems to be working. This can be such a powerless feeling especially when you have experienced the flow of movement. What then? You run around in your head hoping to find some resolve, a glimpse of a solution. This is where we can easily become desperate.

We are suddenly being pulled by all of the things we feel we must do to keep our hologram running. We have a daily routine of actions that we perform to support our reality. Whether we are in business or working for someone else there is always a sense of commitment to a set of conditions we have established to run our reality. Because of this, when those moments of utter "non-movement" occurs, we are thrown completely off course as there is now much uncertainty about the stability of our reality. We fear a collapse of our reality. The question is, *What defines your world?* Exactly what are the conditions by which reality exists for you? We are so involved in running our reality, ensuring its existence according to the model held in our mind, that we do not see the illusion of our beliefs. We are unaware of the story we have told ourselves about why we must operate the way we do, and about the outcome should we choose to operate otherwise.

What I find fascinating is to observe myself in action when I am completely submerged in my story; the story that presents conditions and restrictions on the operation of my reality. It is also fascinating to observe others in their themes, since we each have our own theme by which we run our show. Here are a few themes and mechanics used in playing out these themes:

Focus: RELATIONSHIP ISSUES

These are people who operate reality based on a stream of relationship issues. Not that we all don't experience the challenges of relationships. The difference is that some of us are completely focused on "Why can't I have a good relationship?" "Why can't I find someone who appreciates me?" "Why can't I find the perfect mate?", "Why can't I find a mate?", "I am a good person. Why can't I find someone who appreciates me?" Another offshoot of this is the theory held by some women that because of their success they cannot find a man who is not intimidated by their success. Upholding such concepts only serves to ensure that you will not encounter the appropriate mate. We must examine the truth about what we think of + about ourselves. The relationship conditions encountered are simply showing up to support the story you have told yourself of what you are, who you are and what your deficiencies are, and also what you or can have deserve. There is also fear. The question is, fear of what? There are also men who feel the same way about their success. They have a fear of being taken advantage of and so in this kind of theme this is what they attract. Recurring patterns define a theme. Themes however present us with an opportunity to learn, expand and make different choices.

Focus: STABILITY IN WORKING AND PAYING BILLS

This is an interesting one: I have observed those whose main focus is on maintaining a secure job and paying all their bills. That's it! There is no peripheral vision or risk-taking. Their entire experience is about working and paying the bills. Understand that game players like this are unable to relate to or understand those who operate outside this kind of seemingly stable zone.

Focus: OBSESSIVE SPIRITUAL DISORDER

There are those whose main objective is to save the world from itself. They believe that the world needs to conform to their way of thinking. Such individuals band together with others like themselves in supporting this theme. They become magnets for disorder so that they can fulfill their theme. They actually become the projector of disharmony or non-peace, as they perceive it, in order to fulfill their theme of saving the world. The search for peace further stabilizes a reality/projection of just the opposite. The question is, what have we defined as peace? People kill every day in the name of peace. At this point many of us are recruited into supporting this projection of non-peace as the media so cleverly provide us with the necessary images. Our energy is unsuspectingly [unwittingly?] spent supporting the projections of others which we ultimately buy into in subtle ways, hence the power of religion and spiritual organizations.

Focus: INCESSANT STRUGGLE

For some, struggle is all they know. They do not know what it is to function outside of the realm of incessant struggle. As a matter of fact, they will create conditions to ensure that there is struggle involved. This theme can run through an entire race of people. This, like all patterns, is a challenge to break, especially when one is not aware of being caught in a theme, a pattern, the foundation upon which their reality is built.

Focus: MARTYR

Self-sacrifice or victimization is indeed a theme. There are those who are lifelong martyrs; this is all they know. The payoff for them is the pity received from those around them. They are known as the sacrificial lamb. They are generally quite proud of their role . . . as they should be: It takes tremendous energy to consistently be in this space!

Focus: HEALTH

There are those with endless health issues; just one disorder after another. They do not know how to live without these disorders, just like the rest of us. What would we do if our themes failed us? When we are used to playing this role, it causes great confusion if there is no illness lurking around the corner. Everything in the life of the individual is set up to support this theme. Shifting away from these conditions would mean completely remodeling or demolishing their reality. A new construct would have to be built, and that can be devastating, so at times health issues are resolved and then some time down the road new ones will emerge.

Focus: STRIVING FOR RECOGNITION

Some literally spend their lives working for recognition, hoping that the world will see just how "good" they are, just how talented they are, just how worthy they are. We define the results as "success." The high derived from this journey to recognition is generally short-lived. Shortly after their achievements there is still a sense of deficiency, so they must complete yet an even more worthy accomplishment. This is an endless quest for such beings. Like all other themes there is an original imprint or program that initiated this theme. One has set out on a fool's quest, but still great learning will come from this when one becomes aware of this vicious cycle, after which one can begin to live from a space of creating and achieving for the sheer conscious pleasure of doing so. Make no mistake that we are not enjoying all that we do. There are, however, many levels of experiencing joy.

Focus: MISERY

Yes, there are those who absolutely love misery! These are the complainers. There is never a moment of recognizing the flow within which we all exist. They can be considered the eternal pessimist. There is only doom and gloom and fear. Misery is fear. There is no bright side for such folks and so they will dismiss any such notion presented to them. They are convinced that this is just the way it is for them and they are correct, as they are unable to see outside of their lifelong theme/experience. This is all that they know and anything outside of that only happens to other people. They are committed to their misery just as we are all committed to our themes.

So, getting back to those moments when nothing seems to be working . . . . Well, from the above themes, you have an idea of the short-circuiting that might occur when your game freezes on you. Even if you do not fit into any of the above categories, it matters not, as we all have processes and procedures by which our model of reality is run. We have routine functions in maneuvering or navigating through our physical life. When any of those patterns are compromised we feel helpless and challenged. Why isn't anything working?! Especially when we have become accustomed to things working in a certain format, we know how to generate the same results over and over again; it is tried and true. We know how to meet our needs. Well, what if the rules of our game are changing or have changed for you personally. This kind of change, believe it or not, was initiated by you of course, through your thoughts and desires. The situation, however, is that you did not expect those changes to bring your life to a screeching halt. Old solutions no longer work, old survival strategies no long work; what now? As we stand inside the experience, all we can see is a pending potential for chaos and collapse if we don't get a handle on things. But what does "get a handle on things" mean? What is it we fear will happen and if these things come to pass? What does that mean for you? These are the questions that we must ask ourselves. Remember that whatever format you have been living by has simply been another illusory construct which has supported your game. It has been your dance with the experience we call physical reality. This dance has of course been based on your theme.

Our entire concept of producing currency is skewed from the beginning, especially for those whose entire theme is cradled in the production of money and financial survival. What do I mean by this? Well, we have all developed set conditions by which we limit ourselves to cash/currency production. It's challenging for us to wrap our minds around other possibilities not governed by third-dimensional rules, guidelines and limitations.

To the naked eye, and to the physical processing of emotions, we are fooled into believing that nothing is happening. But what if your life as you have been living it is simply becoming something else? The struggle and fast-paced mind-work that you had operated by is in transition. You are at the crossroads between worlds, making the switch to a more simplified reality. The job that you had no longer exists because for so long you had been wishing for freedom, and a more stress-free way of sustaining your life. Perhaps this is why your job was terminated, perhaps this is why your marriage/relationship ended, perhaps this is why your house is in foreclosure, perhaps this is why you are moving, perhaps this is why your business is failing. The question is, *What did you ask for?* We quickly forget what we had been asking for over the past several years. It is very common for us to continuously verbalize what we no longer want to deal with or experience, but we are not necessarily doing anything about it, at least not consciously. Then suddenly we are hit with change, which feels quite disabling.

When nothing seems to be working it is best not to force the issue with old solutions, especially if there is resistance coming from within. We should honor that signal and simply *stop*. What is further challenging is the feeling that you should be *doing* something. A sense of doom overshadows everything during those moments. Sometimes there is simply nothing to do but to ride it out. We are so conditioned to run our reality from the autopilot self, rather than to let go and move into a space of inner guidance. We have even learned to manipulate that inner guidance, and this has become a familiar mode of comfort experienced by most of us until we become aware of it. Understand that we will experience withdrawals when the standard theme is no longer dictating our movement. We are caught in *unpredictability_*which generates fear; the uncertainty of the next moment. *"When nothing seems to be working:"* this can be a powerful place to be. This is where you completely let go and allow yourself to do nothing, perhaps just sitting and watching a movie or whatever the moment directs you to do. We most often resist engaging in these *true* activities as we feel a sense of betrayal and irresponsibility in not sitting and worrying about our situation. In moments of nothing working this kind of prompting to do nothing with the exception of simple entertainment allows the autopilot self to step out of the way. In stepping away from the autopilot mind and actions we diminish the interference run by the mind like ripples in the ocean. We then stop or slow down the mind chatter and speculations of the future, which can only serve to slow down the unfolding of change, and also runs the risk of creating disabling outcomes through the sheer activation of our imagination.

This entire process of *when nothing seems to be working* is indeed science, though we might not see it as that. Why not? Because we have a standard or set way by which we model everything, and with that we shut out any approach that does not seem to resemble the familiar. It also reminds me of stopping to change the tape or the battery in order to continue filming or recording or whatever that moment of transition requires. This article describes a simple yet significant experience that will generally produce profound results and conclusions regardless which direction we swing towards. So when nothing seems to be working, remember that silence can be the loudest sound you will ever hear, and that the visible world is made up of the invisible world. The particle–wave dance is making quite a splash, reforming, reshaping and rebuilding your personal reality, which you have desired and imagined into existence. So again the question is *What did you ask for?* You may never remember the assortment of desires that you have initiated but rest assured that no matter how it unfolds it's your dream and that moment will pass and activity will resume!

30

Ancestral Imprints

Do we understand what it is that we cling to in clinging to our ancestors? We are in love with the idea of our ancestral past and with that we cling to an idea about a lineage of people who validate our own present existence. There is a comfort felt in being cradled in our history regardless of the extremes expressed by the past. We honor those who have come before us. We honor their journey, their struggles and their triumphs. We believe in our ancestors and with that we hold tightly to the security of those who have come before us.

We own what we cling to in a way that intertwines our very life force. Let me first explain that small portions of our life force is tied into every angle and aspect of those things, thoughts, people and emotions which form the core of our reality. It is the only way that the visual world can exist before us. We infuse it with our life force. Now there are many conditions which affect us, from physical health to emotional health. Our spiritual health is also compromised as a result of depletion in the expansiveness of one's consciousness. This low vibration in consciousness is prolonged by the imprints we are tied into. What are imprints? Where are these imprints? Imprints are a frequency stamp of particular concepts, ideas, beliefs, limitations, diseased thoughts; the subconscious accepts imprints as certainties, impactful frequency patterns with a resonance of permanency and so they become stuck in our consciousness as acceptability's. *acceptabilities?*

The ancestral piece is a touchy subject but one that I have felt necessary to address. Scientists are now able to analyze and read the frequency patterns from our photographs, our hair a flake of skin etc. They can now read the frequency patterns of ancestral health maladies coming from thousands of years back yet traveling through the gene pool. What I have come to realize and would like to share with you is that the DNA alteration which occurred some distant time ago blocked a natural immunizing process which over time as civilizations changed the DNA began to store/record/encode itself with the imprints of disharmonic frequencies which had a disabling impact on the body. This would include emotional imprints able to create a toxic effect on the body especially if the body received this emotional processing as trauma. This would of course create blockages in the body resulting in an inadequate flow of oxygen to the cells resulting in the imprint of specific maladies now formed. These imprints over time begin to compound creating a more compromised immune system.

The world in which we live today is riddled with Bio warfare but the body is no longer able to stand up to this imposition, this war on the immune system. This is known and this is understood by those who seek to control, destroy and reduce the population.

We must now refer to the many levels of ancestral trails as this battle for your mind dates back to pre-planetary life. The continued reference to powerful ones they called Gods is evidence of the extraordinary abilities of these beings who understood inner technology but ensured the imprisonment of human consciousness. In the end it's all about your consciousness. The experiences of our ancestors remain in our consciousness, but most importantly we must face the truth about the tactics implemented in order to ensure the cradling of these imprints. As a matter of fact there are new imprints being added, ones that are extremely impactful, such as the rise in breast cancer, prostate cancer, cervical cancer. Like all diseases and everything else these hold specific frequency patterns, establishing distinctive imprints which will then attach to generations to come. We are the ancestors of the future and you are being used to affect or establish an already planned robotic species in a future in the making.

When we hold on so tightly to the ancestors we must realize that we are holding all of these imprints in the genetic memory and in our individual and collective consciousness. The imprints vary per race of people and racial bloodline. We often times believe that we can never let the past slip away, we often times believe that we must cling to the ways of our ancestors but we are in a different time and it is the reverse, for the ancestors look to you to break the code; to break the cycle. They look to you to break the zombie effect; they look to you to send a ripple back through time and forward into the future. The traumatic experiences of a people such as slavery and the holocaust are greatly imprinted and it is through these strongly infused imprints that all other imprints according to race, culture and ethnicity are being held in place by the minds of the collective.

Again if we wish to honor our ancestors we must release them, we must let them go so that they are free to transcend from the world of death to which we have imprisoned them and idealized them. You are some of your own ancestors who have reincarnated into this time however you will not find freedom as you are still locked into your experiences of the past. You are holding your own self back. The other factor is that the disconnection of the natural immortal ability of the body is tied into the prolonged establishment of these imprints. "Keep them hooked into the imprints of the ancestors because just as long as they do they will never see what's coming".

For the human body to live 250,000 years is not a miracle, neither is it an impossible dream, neither is it a ridiculous idea. Your memory of a life not bound by time was altered and such limiting perceptions took the forefront, streaming such limiting codes from our DNA. Despite this illusion of limitation our DNA remains unlimited in its access beyond time and space; an endless stream of codes and data. We have been bamboozled into believing that a long life will be pointless as we no longer remember that such timeless bodies were occupied by minds capable of building new concepts and new models of this virtual playground. It is the ancestors whom we have no knowledge of that were the magicians of time, masters of their own realities and creators of their own lives, some have sent aspects of their consciousness into this time to remind you of another time, another way, one of unlimited potentials.

For those who are ready to return from the dream, the sleep state, this will ring true in your soul and for others you are perhaps not done with your limitations, for sometimes it's easier to cling to what is believed to be the known as opposed to the unknown. The unknown requires surrender to you; a responsibility to yourself for only then can we stretch forth a helping hand; it is only when we are atop the mountain. You will have forged a way, for the journey of a thousand miles not only begins with one step, it begins with you. Let us honor our ancestors by cracking the code and going beyond, into what might seem to be the impossible.

31

The packaging of Abundance in a Renovated Matrix

There is tremendous distortion around the concept of abundance. It has been understood for quite some time now that we are in the age of enlightenment. It is clear that we are also in the age of abundance according to the current hyped concept to which minds are being herded. People in desperation are jumping on the bandwagon of the next feel good ride without embarking on an in depth understanding of where it all leads. Enlightenment is Abundance and abundance is enlightenment. Do we understand this concept? Many will say that they do but there is much evidence to prove otherwise.

This concept of abundance has been more about money and material gain than the actual expansion of one's natural abilities to align with creation. Enlightenment has been made into a finite concept masked by words and actions that seem to portray an expansion of mind moving beyond matter. Packages of memorized concepts simply become another programming while the individual is routed into another illusion. Such illusions become its own matrix or system under which many will find comfort as the illusion is painted to resemble an expansion of awareness

It is indeed our right to enjoy the physical plane in whatever way we choose. To enjoy our material positions is also our right. We are here to have the full experience of the earth plane. As we progress in this playing field we begin to move towards grander states of consciousness. This grander state of conscious begins to awaken natural abilities that have been forgotten or have been dormant for quite some time. The ability to be in tune or to understand the intricacies of the unfolding of our desires are not realized. The process and the outcome of desires play a major role in the limitations which may be imposed on one's life as well as the impact on the lives of others. This abundance movement simply encourages one to desire without thought or deeper clarity of such choices. Although all experiences present us with an opportunity to expand to understand, the bigger picture will allow the individual to make more expansive choices.

When we set forth a desire we are so anxious to see the manifestation of the desire that any opportunity that comes along many will immediately jump on board viewing this as a sign of the manifestation of your desire. Your decision will bear fruit but sometimes at a cost to yourself and others. Fear and survival becomes the root of our choices. We convince ourselves that the art or science of abundance is working in our favor. On one level this is so as you are being provided with the necessary experience whether it is realized or not. We subtly manipulate the process of manifestation most often without realizing this as we in turn subtly manipulate people and situations to bend the outcome. We then see this as the power of manifestation and not the power of determination supported by manipulation, fear and survival.

There are multitudes of workshops and books promoting mass hypnosis on acquiring money. These seminars are priced in higher increments of currency in order to manipulate followers or the desperate into "manifesting" a way to raise the funds to attend. They in turn are excited to testify that they were miraculously able to scrape the funds together to attend; this is now seen as a sign of pending abundance. This is then supported by the hype received after attending these events. People return with a mantra or programming which plays over and over in their heads of abundance cloaked in an enlightenment speech. One that ensures them of their divine right to happiness while aspects of themselves remain unresolved but rather swept under the rug of the subconscious mind only to resurface when the excitement of the material has died down.

On the other hand there are those who have not been able to see any of their desires manifest and for some it has actually been a blessing. Manifestation under the umbrella of enlightenment will occur without compromise to one's soul. Such compromises operating via the manipulation of others or at the expense of others will become an accrual of debts. The law of balance swings into action as situations ensuring balance begins presenting itself and we in turn begin to feel victimized and despondent. The teacher or facilitator is also affected as his/her own expansion has been stifled. These deceptive approaches or concepts of abundance affect our life force especially when in denial of the impact of the process. Abundance from an enlightened/aware principle occurs when allowed to unfold without the continued focus of the tangible substance of money which serves as a symbol of a quantitative value applied to energy hence the word currency. We are not always ready for those conditions which present themselves for the purpose of balance.

To take it a step further in explanation the current concept of abundance is tied into the "survival program". This survival program operates on a concept of survival at all cost. This is chemically wired into our emotional network. We have however become experts at disguising the emotions of survival which is actually being driven by fear. This allows us to make decisions or choices which we validate through our idea of manifestation. This concept of abundance applies to those in what we view as the "awareness movement" while those who are considered to be unaware are simply living there lives and acknowledging that they are hustling to survive. They are not in denial of it. If they steal or manipulate they are not in denial of it. They are fully aware that this is there mode of operation. It is not camouflaged by anything other than a need to survive.

The question is how different are many of those who are leaders, teachers and practitioners of the new "abundance concept". Is the manner in which the audience is being convinced assessed as a manipulative process, not in all cases of course but in most? Followers have made a choice of their own free will to absorb the concept being shared. To what degree of desperation are many of those eagerly engaged in receiving the information? Is it any different than sales strategies and the psychological manipulation imposed by marketing companies? How many of these gurus have informed the audience of their association with the best marketing geniuses out there. Marketing is all about appealing to deficiencies, needs, wants and desires of individuals and if those aspects do not exist then they are stimulated within the individual. The function of the brain once again is studied and the subconscious is intercepted. The subconscious is rented out and filled with components that will ensure the necessary response.

This current abundance theme is no different than what general consumers are involved in. The general populous is encouraged to establish great credit so that they may obtain financing for just about anything desired regardless of tangible currency. They are however manifesting the things needed by applying for credit whereby they become debtors in the end. They are now indebted and must now ensure continuous payment against this debt. They have become credit worthy in order to become debtors. In this camouflaged concept of abundance people are scrambling to become millionaires and are running off to the nearest seminar being held by anyone who appears to have the formula for producing this finite abundance while one's life force is being depleted. How much time will you have on the planet to spend it? So the race is on.

Again having a monetary flow is your right. It is your right to never go without. We must however examine the process by which we are defining, limiting and harnessing abundance. Abundance is a holistic process. It encompasses the fluidity of energy and our ability to dance with it, to move with it on all levels. It is life itself. It is our ability to be the expression of subatomic particles moving into the atomic realm; the realm of particularized matter not confined to one form but being able to move in and out of the sold world at will. Abundance cannot be measured otherwise it is then a finite experience, one of limitation and finality.

All of our experiences are different yet for each of us it is the process by which we expand into creation. We are gradually being reintroduced to the infiniteness that we are... yet forgotten in order to move through these experiences. Until we understand the substance and source and all that is attached to our desires we will continue to create debts no differently than owning a credit card, a debtor's card. Many times if we were to immediately receive the things that we desire a number of us can attest to the affect that it could potentially have had on our lives or the lives of others in a not so favorable manner. If our experiences are indeed the manner in which we become expansive then your soul ensures the completion of that which is to be understood through experience.

For some of us had we received large sums of money at particular periods in our lives it would have redirected us from specific concepts to be learned or remembered; knowledge that is tied into ones future and the future of other souls. It is important to see the bigger picture of the format of our lives, lay it out on the table like a quilt and review your journey through to this point in time. Review the many amazing things, people, places, your children, and your loved ones that may not have existed had some of your desires come to pass at that moment. Your desire is however falling through time into manifestation based on your journey and your ability to trust the process. Manifestations can however occur immediately according to our understanding of what is being desired. Most often there are attachments to our desires which restrict the unfolding of one's desire to a particular path of manifestation.

As human beings our natural desire is to assist others especially those we are close to but sometimes making them inclusive of your desire is not always in alignment with their journey. Wanting to have a large sum of money to give to the people around you may very well interfere with the individual's growth process as the money becomes a distraction and a Band-Aid for issues or emotional challenges to be worked out by the individual. It is for this reason that many people winning large sums of money generally lose it all in a very short time. Money then becomes the tour guide for the journey. That's another reason why there are so many unhappy financially wealthy people. Abundance is the result of ones journey into one's self; a rediscovery of the infiniteness of one's existence unlimited and uninhibited by time and space. We are no longer settling for illusions of a grander reality. Without this understanding many manipulate the process. We all have at some point. I certainly have and many times paid dearly for what I believed to be a clear manifestation. What people are being sold is a "renovated matrix". The matrix has been repainted, new colors and furniture but it sits on the same foundation, one that is finite, one that will keep you on the reincarnation wheel for you will have created new debts and unable to see beyond the sparkle and the glitter of the new paint and furniture.

The theme of abundance is also tied into finding ones purpose. Understand that your purpose is to allow the manifestation of life and all that you have done, are currently doing and will do, is your purpose. To limit oneself to a particular idea of your purpose is to disqualify all of the joy, pain, trials, tribulations and all things in between which have gifted you with this moment, this expanding being that you are. You have the right to create and experience an unlimited number of purposes. Why limit yourself?

No one said that discovering one's self would be easy and painless, for you are releasing old programs and ideas and replacing them with an organic you. It's called dismantling the survival program because that is what we are all tied into. Fear of inhalation through loss of life, money, material possessions, mind, power etc. Wouldn't you prefer to understand the science of your life, your body, your mind, how to reactivate full brain function, how to see beyond the matrix of this life, how to have an endless life, how to never grow old as time is no longer a finite program in your cells, how to journey to other crevices of existence, how to live beyond your five senses, how to feel the breath of nature as yourself, how to be more than your body and the color of your skin, how to be creation which you already are. That would certainly be an abundant life, experienced through the expansion of one's consciousness, an enlightenment of you as source. If freedom is what you seek then allow yourself to see through the bells and whistles of the matrix. Abundance is your birthright but it's up to you to determine the manner in which you choose to define it! Be holistically wealthy!

32

The Beauty of the Game

After all is said and done there is beauty in the human experience. There is splendor in the dance. At what point do we begin to feel the humor and excitement in moving about on planet earth? Memory is our ticket into a more pleasurable experience. To remember is to reassume sovereignty while setting aside the illusion of imprisonment. We stand at the brink of an opportunity to take real flight once again, unlimited and uninhibited by the magic spell cast oh so long ago.

The games we have played; race wars, religious wars, cultural wars, political wars, competitive wars, the gender war and oh so many disharmonic themes; all are essential parts of discovery, the anthology of the expedition. When we begin to ask questions which go deeper than common shallow views, it is a sign that we are being stirred to return from our position as sleepers and pawns in the game. It is a sign of accomplishment. We have discovered life and we have discovered death as we have danced in the valley of both. When there is a sense of having wrung the human experience dry, then perhaps it's time to create something new.

The great realization is that although we have been operating in the slowest timeline, we have amassed a wealth of knowledge, having journeyed the highs, lows and in-betweens of the stage-one human experience. The value of this is immeasurable; it takes great courage to journey into this field of forgetfulness and accumulates data for the overall expansion of the whole. You have gathered a record of experiences, which could not be calculated out of mere speculation, but gained only through emotion. To feel, to taste, to have your consciousness integrated into the dream, into the matrix, is an amazing feat of bravery. Relationships have been the medium for gathering data on the journey. It is through our relationships with one another that we have been able to weave these emotional experiences. We engage in relationships with both animate and inanimate objects. It is through the joy, the pain, the anger, the love, the bitterness, survival, struggle, the caring, the selfishness, the unselfishness, the competition, the horror, the thrill, all of which we have willingly gifted to each other's lives. Without the unselfish sacrifice of our brothers and sisters we could not have experienced the splendor of the game in this playing field of the great cosmic dance.

The intimacy experienced between masculine and feminine polarities, although miniscule in comparison to the more expansive cosmic orgasmic experience, has allowed us a taste of the ongoing explosion that continues to birth creation endlessly. Through relationships of the heart we touch the core of our souls; we tap into the core of creation as our bodies echo the rhythmic formula seen throughout life. As we breathe in and breathe out, we form a vortex where two points meet as energy spins at opposite ends and comes together. Bodies move in and out, coming together in further expression of the point zero effect where antigravity points, also known as vortex points, are formed. It is at point zero, the point of no-spin, that we create. From point zero all unfolds in creation, and so it is with our movement in physical intimacy as we bring forth life. We have never stopped embodying and reiterating the great formula. How could we? In our descent into matter we have simply reduced the infiniteness of ourselves to an essence, a much reduced vibration of who we are in the vastness of the unlimited. The secret is that we are the sum total of this diminished essence. When this realization comes home to us there is laughter as we can now see and enjoy the comedy of our blindness and forgetfulness.

It is a realization that there is nothing out there, but that it is all happening in a deep aspect of mind, collective agreements of optical illusions seated next to our created private realities. We validate each other's' existences, we validate each other's dreams, we are therefore important to one another despite our reduced feelings for others in our lives. What profound love, what profound allowing, and what beautiful sacrifice, for without these amazing players your journey would not have unfolded the way it has. Every moment of all of your experiences has lead you to this glorious moment, a moment of discovery, for perhaps it's time to return home to who you are. What worlds will you create after this one? What will you imagine into existence in another potential of time? You are a melody playing endlessly as an echo throughout creation. You are felt in all potentials of time. You are time itself. You are what you seek. Again I feel a profound love for the journey and the many aspects of myself that you are; I am you and you are I.

Death is but an illusion, an un-mastered aspect of the journey. You're coming home without falling into the previously experienced booby traps and dead ends requires your mastery or reintegration of the atomic field; matter will no longer appear as a barrier or ruler of your movement through space and time. Decay and old age will be but a memory, simply an essential experience in the matrix. The matrix operates on temporal principles in order for you to return again and again to the experience. You are timeless. You have the ability to regulate the molecular structure of your body, moving beyond the illusion of the system of limitation designed for the human experience. Gravity is your fear yet it exists as a strong defining point in the matrix. It is a reminder of our physical limitations, our inability to defy the laws of physics that we have come to accept as a truth. We defined the laws of physics by which we would move about in the system. Now we must redefine who we are beyond the old operating programs stored in our biology, our consciousness and our perception.

The game is beautiful once we allow ourselves to re-member. Only then will we enjoy being here on a much grander level. The transition can be painful and challenging and not for the faint of heart, but you must ask yourself just how many more times are you willing to re-live this limited existence you have created. There is no rush, for ultimately at some point in time we will all return home to conscious awareness of who we are as co-creators. As the old programs fade away, our lives change and everything around us changes. Pain comes as we experience symptoms of withdrawal from the chemical addictions and bonds formed between ourselves and people, places, things, experiences and personalities which have shaped our identity. By our own choosing and desire to regain memory we pull away from the formula of the matrix. We can no longer be the same. We must weather the illusionary obstacles in our path, as they present themselves. However, we need only change our perception to utilize these obstacles as opportunities to grow stronger and more self-assured in who we are. These moments will pass, but at times there will be a desire to return to the old as an escape from the pending difficulties that appear to be before you. Attempting to go back will only result in intense difficulties, as what you left behind was only an illusion, which you are now attempting to re-create, an illusion whose time has passed. The possibility of expansion stands before us, as we unfold and we activate ourselves into these amazing dimensional vehicles that our bodies already are; for those entering this kind of awareness. Such an evolution is open to everyone, but will only be experienced by those who choose to move forward. Moving towards a deep level of sovereignty will require taking responsibility for one's self, such beings will begin to make discoveries not yet seen by science. These are natural abilities that will manifest for each of us once the blinders of subservience and dependency are removed. You are a divine cosmic scientist whose abilities will far exceed what this stage-one matrix has to offer.

Oh yes, it's been a beautiful journey, and we have only just begun. Just simply allow yourself to be what you already are!

Notes

Article 5

(1) Brain Plasticity and Cognition by Kolb, B., Muhammad, A., & Gibb, R., Searching for factors underlying cerebral plasticity in the normal and injured brain, Journal of Communication Disorders (2010), doi:10.1016/j.jcomdis.2011.04.007

Article 8

(1) Kelly Roper, Horoscope Group Editor
http://horoscopes.lovetoknow.com/Astrological_Houses

Article 13

(1) IMF calls for dollar alternative by Ben Rooney
http://money.cnn.com/2011/02/10/markets/dollar/index.ht
m

(2) Schrödinger's Cat
http://en.wikipedia.org/wiki/Schr%C3%B6dinger%27s_cat
There is a workshop planned for FEBRUARY 19, 2011- MONEY & THE SCARCITY AND PLENTY GAME; *How the brain responds to the illusion of money*

CPSIA information can be obtained
at www.ICGtesting.com
Printed in the USA
FSOW02n0306270116
16244FS